EXODUS FROM EGYPT

Moses and God's Mercy

JOHN MACARTHUR

THOMAS NELSON
Since 1798

NASHVILLE   DALLAS   MEXICO CITY   RIO DE JANEIRO

Published in Nashville, Tennessee, by Thomas Nelson. Thomas Nelson is a trademark of Thomas Nelson, Inc.

Layout, design, and writing assistance by Gregory C. Benoit Publishing, Old Mystic, CT.

Thomas Nelson, Inc. titles may be purchased in bulk for educational, business, fund-raising, or sales promotional use. For information, please e-mail *SpecialMarkets@ThomasNelson.com.*

Scripture quotations are taken from THE NEW KING JAMES VERSION. Copyright © 1982 by Thomas Nelson, Inc. Used by permission. All rights reserved.

ISBN 978-1-4185-3325-0

Printed in the United States of America

13 14 15 QG 0 9

Contents

~ ⌒ ~

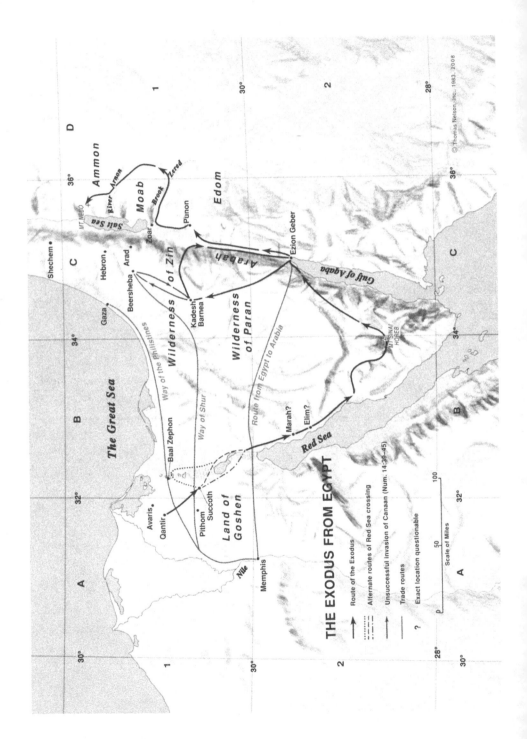

THE EXODUS FROM EGYPT

Route of the Exodus

Alternate routes of Red Sea crossing

Unsuccessful invasion of Canaan (Num. 14:39-45)

Trade routes

? Exact location questionable

Scale of Miles
0   50   100

The Great Sea

Shechem

Gaza

Hebron

Arad

Beersheba

Kadesh Barnea

Wilderness of Zin

Wilderness of Paran

Way of the Philistines

Way of Shur

Route from Egypt to Arabia

Baal Zephon

Avaris

Qantir

Pithom

Succoth

Land of Goshen

Memphis

Nile

Marah?

Elim?

Red Sea

MT. SINAI/HOREB

Gulf of Aqaba

Arabah

Ezion Geber

Edom

Punon

Zoar

Salt Sea

MT. NEBO

Moab

Ammon

River Arnon

Brook Zered

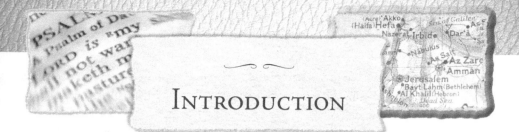

INTRODUCTION

The people of Israel lived in Egypt for 430 years, and most of that time was spent in slavery. The Lord, however, had promised Abraham that his descendants would be led out of their slavery and back into the land of Canaan, and our studies begin when that time had arrived. The Lord began leading His people out of Egypt by selecting a man to lead them: Moses, one of the most humble men in Scripture.

During their travels toward Canaan, the people of Israel witnessed the power and faithfulness of God in countless ways. He went with them physically in a pillar of cloud and a pillar of fire; He met with Moses face to face on Mount Sinai; He provided food and water and delivered the people from the most deadly army on earth. Yet despite all these miracles and many more, the people of Israel constantly grumbled and complained against God and Moses.

In these twelve studies, we will jump back and forth in chronological history, looking at one historical period and then skipping forward or backward in time as needed. We will examine God's calling of Moses, the ten plagues on Egypt, the Ten Commandments to His people, and much more. But through it all, we will also learn some precious truths about the character of God, and we will see His great faithfulness in keeping His promises. We will learn, in short, what it means to walk by faith.

ᴥ What We'll Be Studying ᴥ

This study guide is divided into four distinct sections in which we will examine selected Bible passages:

Section 1: History. In this first section, we will focus on the historical setting of our Bible text. These five lessons will give a broad overview of the people, places, and events that are important to this study. They will also provide the background for the next two sections. This is our most purely historical segment, focusing simply on what happened and why.

Section 2: Characters. The four lessons in this section will give us an opportunity to zoom in on the characters from our Scripture passages. Some of these people were introduced in section 1, but in this part of the study guide we will take a much closer look at these personalities. Why did God see fit to include them in His Book in the first place? What made them unique? What can we learn from their lives? In this practical section, we will answer all of these questions and more, as we learn how to live wisely by emulating the wisdom of those who came before us.

SECTION 3: THEMES. Section 3 consists of two lessons in which we will consider some of the broader themes and doctrines touched on in our selected Scripture passages. This is the guide's most abstract portion, wherein we will ponder specific doctrinal and theological questions that are important to the church today. As we ask what these truths mean to us as Christians, we will also look for practical ways to base our lives upon God's truth.

SECTION 4: SUMMARY AND REVIEW. In our final section, we will look back at the principles that we have discovered in the scriptures throughout this study guide. These will be our "takeaway" principles, those which permeate the Bible passages that we have studied. As always, we will be looking for ways to make these truths a part of our everyday lives.

⤳ ABOUT THE LESSONS ⤳

⤐ Each study begins with an introduction that provides the background for the selected Scripture passages.

⤐ To assist you in your reading, a section of notes—a miniature Bible commentary of sorts—offers both cultural information and additional insights.

⤐ A series of questions is provided to help you dig a bit deeper into the Bible text.

⤐ Overriding principles brought to light by the Bible text will be studied in each lesson. These principles summarize a variety of doctrines and practical truths found throughout the Bible.

⤐ Finally, additional questions will help you mine the deep riches of God's Word and, most importantly, to apply those truths to your own life.

Section 1:

History

In This Section:

∾ I ∾
THE SELECTION OF MOSES

∾ HISTORICAL BACKGROUND ∾

(Read Exodus 1–2 for background on Moses' life.) The Israelites (the "Hebrews") had been living in Egypt for more than four hundred years. They had been slaves for much of that time. But even during their slavery, the Lord had blessed His people, and their numbers grew dramatically. In fact, they became so numerous that Pharaoh, the ruler of Egypt, began to fear that they would become a threat to his nation, so he devised a murderous plan: all males born to the Hebrews would be put to death immediately after being born. Quickly this evil king set his plan in motion. He would put an end to the Hebrew race!

But the Lord had other ideas. First, He caused the Egyptian midwives to lie to the king. They told him that the Hebrew women were so strong that they gave birth *without* the midwives' aid. Then God used Pharaoh's wicked act to move one very significant Hebrew baby—Moses—into the house of Pharaoh himself.

Moses was brought up in the royal Egyptian court. This provided him with a top-notch education, exposure to the highest levels of government, and connections within the king's court. It also removed him from the hardships of his people—for a time. But the Lord did not permit him to become complacent in his role, and He never let Moses forget that he, too, was a Hebrew.

One day, Moses saw an Egyptian slave driver abusing a Hebrew, and he intervened, killing the Egyptian and burying him in the sand. But his deed did not go unnoticed. So, fearing for his life, he then fled into the wilderness and started a new life in Midian, where he married and settled down to live comfortably as a shepherd.

But again, the Lord had other plans. He had ordained all the circumstances of Moses' life, preparing him for one momentous task: leading the Israelites out of bondage and into the promised land. This would be an intimidating and costly calling for Moses, but the Lord would be with him each step of the way.

The Burning Bush: *While his fellow Hebrews had been toiling under cruel Egyptian taskmasters, Moses had spent forty years working as a shepherd. All of that was about to change.*

1. Moses: Moses was born a Hebrew in Egypt, but had been raised in the household of Pharaoh, where he had received the very best education and upbringing in the world of his day. "Now it came to pass in those days, when Moses was grown, that he went out to his brethren and looked at their burdens. And he saw an Egyptian beating a Hebrew, one of his brethren. So . . . he killed the Egyptian and hid him in the sand" (Exodus 2:11–12). Moses then fled Egypt, met a priest in Midian, and married his daughter Zipporah. He lived comfortably in Midian for forty years. This is where our study begins.

Horeb, the mountain of God: Mount Sinai, located in the mountainous region between the Red Sea and the Gulf of Aqaba. (See the map in the Introduction.)

2. the Angel of the Lord: This phrase appears frequently throughout Exodus. It describes what is called a *theophany*, a "pre-incarnate appearance" of God prior to the birth of Christ.

the bush was burning with fire, but the bush was not consumed: Moses' attention was drawn to a most unusual sight, that of a burning bush that was not being burnt up by the fire within its branches. Even more amazing, for Moses, was the fact that God would address him through this bush.

3. I will now turn aside and see this great sight: Scholars have attempted to find some natural explanation for the burning bush, such as certain types of flowers with gaseous pods. But Moses had been working in that desert region for forty years and would have been well familiar with the regional flora. He certainly would not have commented on something mundane. This incident was so unusual that he stopped what he was doing to investigate further. A supernatural event is the only viable explanation.

God Speaks to Moses: *The Lord Himself was present at the burning bush, and He spoke directly to Moses to outline His plans.*

5. Do not draw near this place: God's presence is utterly holy, and He will not permit sinful man to draw near Him. We will see this throughout the Israelites' interactions with God; those who approached Him casually risked being struck dead. Christians today have the privilege of entering boldly into His presence, but this is only because we do so through the redeeming blood of Christ.

6. THE GOD OF ABRAHAM, THE GOD OF ISAAC, AND THE GOD OF JACOB: The Lord promised Abraham that He would make a great nation of him, with descendants that outnumbered the stars in the sky (Genesis 15:5). But He also said, "Your descendants will be strangers in a land that is not theirs, and will serve them, and they will afflict them four hundred years. And also the nation whom they serve I will judge; afterward they shall come out with great possessions" (vv. 13–14). Moses did not know it yet, but he was about to participate in the fulfillment of that promise by leading the descendants of Abraham out of Egypt.

MOSES HID HIS FACE, FOR HE WAS AFRAID TO LOOK UPON GOD: We will see this theme reiterated throughout our studies. Moses would later ask to see God's glory, but the Lord would warn him that no one may see His face and live. Moses would also spend time in the Lord's presence in days to come. His own face would glow so brightly that he would have to wear a veil.

7. I KNOW THEIR SORROWS: The Israelites' circumstances were not a surprise to God. As we have already seen, He knew what their situation would be long before it happened, and it was all part of His plan, which He had established "before the foundation of the world" (Ephesians 1:4). Nevertheless, He was still paying close attention to His people's circumstances, and His heart was moved by their plight. He had sent them to Egypt for a purpose, He had sustained them in their bondage, and He would be faithful to carry them back to Canaan.

MOSES' FIRST EXCUSE: *Moses understandably felt inadequate for the great assignment God was giving him. But the Lord promised to overcome his weaknesses.*

11. WHO AM I THAT I SHOULD GO?: On the one hand, Moses was making a realistic assessment of himself: he had been away from Egypt for forty years, living in the desert regions as a shepherd, a class of people despised by the Egyptians (Genesis 46:33–34). On the other hand, however, the Lord had specifically ordained events in Moses' life that would prepare him for his leadership role, including growing up in Pharaoh's household, where he had the best possible education and learned courtly etiquette. This also gave him an access to Pharaoh's court that no other Hebrew had, since he was remembered there.

12. I WILL CERTAINLY BE WITH YOU: God made this same promise to Abraham, Isaac, and Jacob, and He fulfilled it beyond their expectations. He had consistently proven Himself faithful to His Word and to His people, and this promise alone should have been sufficient to give Moses confidence.

13. WHAT IS HIS NAME? : Here Moses raised another objection. Israel might ask for God's name to validate that Moses had been sent by the God of their fathers. Significantly, the question was not "Who is this God?" The Hebrews knew the name *Yahweh* (which Genesis well indicates). Asking "who" would be inquiring about title, name, and identity, whereas "what" inquired into the character, quality, or essence of a person. Thus, God answered Moses' question by pointing to His divine, eternal character.

14. I AM WHO I AM: The almighty God, who created all that exists, is beyond the comprehension of mankind. He always was, always is, and always shall be, and He is unchanging and unfathomable. He is who He is.

22. YOU SHALL PLUNDER THE EGYPTIANS: The Lord laid out for Moses all that would happen before Pharaoh released the Israelites, including the fact that the people would leave Egypt carrying great wealth from their former slave masters. This may have seemed far-fetched to Moses at the time, but it was in keeping with the very promise God had given to Abraham hundreds of years earlier: "The nation whom they serve I will judge; afterward they shall come out with great possessions" (Genesis 15:14).

⌁ READING EXODUS 4:1–17 ⌁

A SERIES OF MIRACULOUS SIGNS: *The Lord gives Moses several dramatic signs with which to prove that he is speaking the words of God.*

1. BUT SUPPOSE: The Lord had revealed many things to Moses at this point. He had told Moses His name, despite the boldness of the request. He had divulged many details of the future, including the fact that the Israelites would eventually leave Egypt with great wealth. And most significantly, the Lord had promised Moses that He would be with him and give him the ability to accomplish the great task of leading His people out of bondage. He had patiently answered each of Moses' questions, offering him reassurances in the face of his hesitancy—but here Moses crossed the line into unbelief.

THE LORD HAS NOT APPEARED TO YOU: God had already told Moses that the people would *not* respond this way; the elders would heed his voice (Genesis 3:18). From a human perspective, however, it is easy to understand Moses' concerns. There is no record that the Lord had appeared to the Israelites during their entire time in Egypt, a period of more than four centuries.

3. IT BECAME A SERPENT: The devil used a literal serpent in the garden of Eden to deceive Eve into eating the forbidden fruit. Here the Lord demonstrated His power over the devil and his evil forces by having His servant cast the serpent to the ground, then pick it up by the tail without being bitten. The miracle showed Moses that God can use anything—even the very wickedness of Satan—to further His own purposes.

6. HIS HAND WAS LEPROUS: Leprosy can give us a picture of sin, as the smallest spot of the disease spreads throughout the body and infects everything it touches. This miracle prefigured some of the plagues that would be sent upon Egypt.

MORE EXCUSES: *The Lord has provided dramatic signs and promises to encourage Moses in his work, but Moses is still not satisfied.*

10. I AM NOT ELOQUENT, NEITHER BEFORE NOR SINCE YOU HAVE SPOKEN TO YOUR SERVANT, BUT AM SLOW OF SPEECH AND . . . TONGUE: This is a very bold statement for Moses to make to God—indeed, it is almost accusatory, suggesting that in all His miracles, God had failed to heal Moses' speech defects. Adam used a similar ploy when God confronted him with his sin, suggesting that somehow his failure was God's fault: "The woman whom *You* gave to be with me, she gave me of the tree, and I ate" (Genesis 3:12, emphasis added). Moses was trying to find excuses for not obeying God, and his final attempt was to blame God Himself.

11. WHO HAS MADE MAN'S MOUTH?: The Lord sometimes used rhetorical questions when confronting mankind's impudence. (See Job 38.)

12. I WILL BE WITH YOUR MOUTH: The Lord had been immensely patient with Moses' excuses, promising again and again that He would work through even Moses' weaknesses and shortcomings. "But when they deliver you up, do not worry about how or what you should speak. For it will be given to you in that hour what you should speak; for it is not you who speak, but the Spirit of your Father who speaks in you" (Matthew 10:19–20).

13. BUT HE SAID: Moses finally made his intentions clear: his previous concerns were merely excuses to cover the fact that he simply did not want to do what the Lord was commanding him to do. His final answer here was, "No! Send someone else!"

14. THE ANGER OF THE LORD WAS KINDLED AGAINST MOSES: God had been patient with Moses' concerns, and He had extended grace and encouragement repeatedly. But He will not withhold His anger indefinitely when His people persist in refusing to obey His word.

AARON . . . YOUR BROTHER: The Lord finally sent both Moses and Aaron to lead His people out of slavery, but this was a concession to Moses' stubbornness rather than the Lord's original intention. Aaron would prove to be both an asset and a liability to Moses' leadership.

16. YOU SHALL BE TO HIM AS GOD: That is, the Lord would speak to Moses directly, and Moses would tell Aaron what to say. This was the pattern throughout the wilderness wanderings after the people left Egypt.

ᕙ FIRST IMPRESSIONS ᕗ

1. *If you had been in Moses' position, how would you have responded to God's command to lead the Israelites out of Egypt?*

2. *What were Moses' fears and concerns? How did the Lord answer those issues?*

3. *How had the Lord prepared Moses for this big assignment? How did He sovereignly use circumstances and "chance events" (humanly speaking) for that purpose?*

4.   *What was Moses giving up by obeying God's command? What did his obedience cost him? What did he gain? See Hebrews 11:23–29.*

⌁ Some Key Principles ⌁

God does not tell us to do things that we cannot accomplish.

Moses apparently suffered from some sort of speech defect. He may have stuttered, as traditional Jewish writers have suggested, or he may simply have felt that he was not very eloquent. Whatever the cause, he was convinced that he could not fulfill the great assignment God was calling him to perform.

Yet the Lord promised him, at each objection, that He would strengthen Moses' weakness and overcome his shortcomings. "Have I not made your mouth?" the Lord asked. "Do I not know your strengths and weaknesses? It is *My* power, not yours, which shall set my people free."

The Lord may sometimes call His children to tasks that seem beyond our ability. What we must remember is that it is not we who are at work, but the power of His Holy Spirit within us. He can use even our very weaknesses to bring about His glory, and He will never call us to do something that we cannot do with His help.

The Lord wants our obedience, not our excuses.

This does not mean that we should not pour out our concerns before the Lord. Moses certainly had some legitimate questions and concerns, such as what he should say and how he would establish his credentials. The Lord patiently addressed those concerns and repeatedly promised him that He would work out the details—that He would, in fact, be right beside Moses each step of the way.

But Moses' real concern had less to do with his inadequacy than with his desires: he simply didn't *want* to obey. He certainly had reasons for not wanting to return to Egypt. He had killed a man there and might still face arrest. He had established a comfortable

11

life in Midian, working for his father-in-law as a shepherd. There is no question that the Lord was calling him to uproot himself and get out of his "comfort zone." And when the Lord calls us, our job is to obey—even if it seems inconvenient or unfamiliar.

When the Lord calls you to do something difficult, be honest in prayer and pour out your fears and concerns before His throne of grace. But once you have expressed your concerns, the final step is to obey. God will provide the power to accomplish what He asks.

The Lord accomplishes great things through weak people.

This is the corollary to the previous principle: once we obey, the Lord will use us to accomplish great things for His eternal kingdom. Moses was learning the lesson that it is God's power, not man's, that accomplishes His miraculous plans. What is required of His people is an obedient spirit, not a roster of tremendous gifts and abilities.

The Lord worked several miracles for Moses, turning his shepherd's crook into a serpent and causing his hand to become leprous and then immediately healing it again. But those miracles were nothing compared to the mighty signs and wonders that the Lord would show in Egypt and in the wilderness through Moses—once he obeyed.

The important thing to remember is that it is God's power, not our own, that accomplishes His plan. In fact, He sometimes uses people who are underequipped, from a human perspective, specifically to show forth *His* power in their lives. "But God has chosen the foolish things of the world to put to shame the wise, and . . . the weak things of the world to put to shame the things which are mighty; and the base things of the world and the things which are despised God has chosen, and the things which are not, to bring to nothing the things that are, that no flesh should glory in His presence" (1 Corinthians 1:27–29).

⌁ Digging Deeper ⌁

5. At what point did Moses' questions go from legitimate concerns to simple stubbornness? How can we distinguish between these two responses in our own hearts?

6. Why did God use the three miracles (snake, leprosy, turning water into blood) to encourage Moses? What did they reveal about God's character?

7. How was Moses' mission affected by the fact that Aaron would be his spokesman? Did Moses' stubbornness interfere with God's sovereign plans?

8. When has God called you to do something that was "outside your comfort zone"? How did you respond to that calling?

9. Is the Lord calling you to some difficult act of obedience at present? Are you making excuses or moving forward in obedience?

10. When have you seen the Lord work through or around your own weaknesses? How has He been glorified by your obedience?

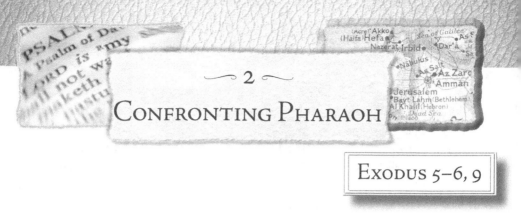

CONFRONTING PHARAOH

2

ᨲ HISTORICAL BACKGROUND ᨲ

Moses returned to Egypt, as the Lord commanded him, and his brother, Aaron, met him along the way—just as God had predicted at the burning bush. The two of them went immediately to the elders of Israel and told them what the Lord had commanded, showing them the signs that the Lord had given Moses—and they believed and rejoiced, just as the Lord had foretold.

But the battle was not over—in fact, it had not even begun. Moses and Aaron still had to face Pharaoh and demand that he release his slaves, and this was not going to be an easy task. Pharaoh was the most powerful man in the world, and he ruled with absolute authority. The Egyptians believed that the Pharaoh ("Pharaoh" is a title, not a proper name) was descended from the gods and that he spoke with divine authority on earth. The Hebrews, on the other hand, were mere slaves, people of utterly no account in Egypt. Yet God had called a lowly Hebrew to approach the greatest man on earth—one who thought he was a god—and tell him that the true God of his slaves commanded him to set them free!

The Lord had told Moses in advance that Pharaoh would not be open to this idea and that he would deliberately "harden his heart" against God's words. But He had also informed Moses that He would use Pharaoh's stubbornness to show forth His glory to the world and that in the end He would redeem His people out of bondage. Yet despite this promise, it still proved a test of faith for Israel and for Moses when the time actually arrived.

ᨲ READING EXODUS 5:1–6:9 ᨲ

LET MY PEOPLE GO: *Moses and Aaron had told the Israelites what the Lord had said to Moses. Now it was time to tell Pharaoh.*

1. AFTERWARD: Moses and Aaron had gone to the elders of the Israelites to tell them the words of the Lord and to perform the signs the Lord had given Moses (see

Study 1). "So the people believed; and when they heard that the LORD had visited the children of Israel and that He had looked on their affliction, then they bowed their heads and worshiped" (Exodus 4:31).

2. WHO IS THE LORD? : The Pharaohs of Egypt believed themselves to be descended from their pagan god Ra. Therefore, Pharaoh thought it beneath his dignity to humble himself before the God of the Israelite slaves. His sad inquiry, "Why should I obey His voice?" would soon be resoundingly answered as the Lord sent devastating plagues upon Egypt. Yet even then, Pharaoh would refuse to humble himself before the almighty God.

4. WHY DO YOU TAKE THE PEOPLE FROM THEIR WORK? : Pharaoh obstinately held to his view that the Hebrews were slackers, using Moses' religious request as a ruse to avoid their slave labors. Even in the midst of horrific plagues that demonstrated the reality of God's presence among His people, Pharaoh stubbornly refused to believe the truth of their claims.

THE LAST STRAW: *Pharaoh reacts with anger, openly rejecting the lordship of Jehovah. Instead, he increases the slaves' workload.*

7. STRAW TO MAKE BRICK: Straw was an essential ingredient in Egyptian brick making, as it was the bonding agent that held the clay together.

8. YOU SHALL LAY ON THEM THE QUOTA OF BRICKS WHICH THEY MADE BEFORE: This was a cruel and harsh response. The people would now have an extra task that they did not have previously—the very time- and energy-consuming task of gathering straw. It effectively doubled their efforts, yet they were still responsible for the same number of bricks at the end of the day!

9. LET THEM NOT REGARD FALSE WORDS: Pharaoh presents an excellent picture of the world's system, which continually rejects the Word of God. He was telling the Israelites that they were fools for believing in the Lord's words through His servant Moses. They were much better off, he claimed, to accept the religious system around them and not chase after fables. Again, Pharaoh would obstinately insist upon this false claim even in the midst of the most incontrovertible proof of God's presence with Israel.

14. THE OFFICERS OF THE CHILDREN OF ISRAEL . . . WERE BEATEN: The Jewish officers probably had grown accustomed to slightly better conditions and treatment than their fellow Hebrews, but they did not escape Pharaoh's wrath. When the world sets itself to oppose the Word of God, all of God's people come under attack.

The people of Israel respond to their suffering by blaming Moses for meddling in their affairs. This will become an unfortunate pattern.

21. you have made us abhorrent in the sight of Pharaoh: The Hebrew leaders were very quick to blame Moses and Aaron for their present suffering—even though they had recently endorsed their authority from the Lord. This sad behavior would be modeled again and again as the Israelites made their way toward Canaan.

22. why have You brought trouble on this people?: The Lord had warned Moses that Pharaoh would harden his heart and refuse to let the people leave (Exodus 3:19–22). The Lord frequently permits His people to experience times of suffering while His plan is unfolding, but He is still entirely in control of all events.

23. neither have You delivered Your people at all: Moses spoke as though he had expected Pharaoh to release the Israelites overnight, but the Lord had warned him in advance that some struggle would be involved. In fact, the struggle had barely even begun at this point! Yet once the Lord's glory was revealed, the tussle itself would seem insignificant and very brief. Centuries later, the apostle Paul would agree: "For I consider that the sufferings of this present time are not worthy to be compared with the glory which shall be revealed in us" (Romans 8:18). And Peter would write, "Beloved, do not think it strange concerning the fiery trial which is to try you, as though some strange thing happened to you; but rejoice to the extent that you partake of Christ's sufferings, that when His glory is revealed, you may also be glad with exceeding joy" (1 Peter 4:12–13).

I am the Lord: *The Lord calls the Israelites to change their focus from their sufferings to His character. He is always faithful, even in times of suffering.*

6:1. Now you shall see what I will do to Pharaoh: The Lord had told Moses at the burning bush that His strength would be revealed through Moses' weaknesses. The same would be true of the sufferings of the Israelites: when they were most sorely oppressed, the Lord would reveal the strength of His arm on their behalf.

he will drive them out of his land: By the time the plagues finished ravaging Egypt, Pharaoh would not merely consent to the Israelites' leaving—he would *drive* them out. And they would leave laden with all the riches of their former slave masters.

2. I am the Lord: When the people of Israel were most discouraged and their hearts were failing, the Lord reminded them of His character. He is the Lord, Creator of heaven and earth, all-powerful yet merciful and loving toward His people. In times of sorrow, the best source of strength and encouragement is to be reminded of God's true nature.

3. BY MY NAME LORD I WAS NOT KNOWN TO THEM: The patriarchs did know the name Yahweh (or Jehovah), but they had not known the fullness of His character. Each of them—Abraham, Isaac, Jacob, and their forebears—had been admitted into some element of communion and intimacy with God, but Moses and his people would be given yet a new glimpse of the character of God as He wrought great miracles on their behalf. When they got outside of Egypt, God Himself would go with them in visible form: a pillar of fire by night, a great cloud of covering by day. He would teach them to build the tabernacle and the ark of the covenant; He would speak to them personally on Mount Sinai. In this way and others, God was going to reveal Himself more fully and personally to the people of Israel.

4. I HAVE ALSO ESTABLISHED MY COVENANT WITH THEM: The Lord had repeatedly promised Abraham and his descendants that they would one day inherit the land of Canaan. (See Genesis 15, for example.)

5. I HAVE ALSO HEARD THE GROANING OF THE CHILDREN OF ISRAEL: The Israelites were accusing God of oppressing them through Pharaoh's "no-straw" decree, but the truth was just the opposite. He heard their cries and felt their suffering, and He would not fail to deliver them in keeping with His promises.

7. THEN YOU SHALL KNOW: The Lord does not want His people to be content with mere "head knowledge" concerning His character—He wants us to experience His regenerating power and grace firsthand. The same was true for the Israelites, who were about to experience God's saving power in their physical deliverance from Egypt.

9. THEY DID NOT HEED MOSES: The people of Israel refused to place their faith in God's promises, because they were entirely focused upon their present sufferings. Today, during such times, it is imperative that we place our faith in God's Word, remembering that these present trials are very temporary but God's glory is eternal.

⤳ READING EXODUS 9:1–35 ⤴

THE PLAGUES: *By now the Lord had already sent four plagues on Egypt. In this section we will look at three more. Each plague provided Pharaoh another chance to repent.*

1. THEN THE LORD SAID TO MOSES: The Lord had already sent the first four plagues on Egypt: waters turned to blood (Exodus 7:20); frogs (8:6); lice (8:17); and flies (8:24). In each case, Pharaoh hardened his heart and refused to heed the word of the Lord.

3. A VERY SEVERE PESTILENCE: The Lord sent a series of devastating plagues on the nation of Egypt, each time demonstrating that He was all-powerful and each time giving Pharaoh an opportunity to voluntarily obey His commands. Many of the specific plagues were also associated with various Egyptian deities. For example, the frog was honored as the special representative of an Egyptian goddess; flies were associated with several of their gods; and the sun, completely eclipsed in the ninth plague, was associated with their greatest god, Ra.

4. THE LORD WILL MAKE A DIFFERENCE: God also demonstrated His faithfulness to His people by sending devastation upon the entire nation of Egypt, while protecting His own people in Goshen from suffering at all. It is worth noting that He did this only with certain plagues, while with others He permitted His people to suffer along with the Egyptians. There are times when the Lord allows His people to suffer, but He will never permit us to suffer true devastation—Christians will never undergo the wrath of God.

5. THE LORD APPOINTED A SET TIME: The Scriptures frequently tell us that God has appointed set times for all things. He is absolutely in control of all that happens in creation, and when His set time arrives, nothing can prevent His plan from moving forward.

6. ALL THE LIVESTOCK OF EGYPT DIED: That is, all that were "in the field" (Exodus 9:3), as opposed to any that were contained inside some structure. The Egyptians venerated cattle, especially bulls, and one of their goddesses was represented as part cow.

7. THEN PHARAOH SENT: Pharaoh had been told that previous plagues had miraculously spared the Israelites, but this time he investigated himself to see if the reports were true. His findings—proving that the Word of the Lord was indeed truth—should have led him to humble himself and submit to God, but he merely hardened his heart still further. When a man hardens himself against the Word of God, he willfully turns truth into falsehood, and vice versa. "Woe to those who call evil good, and good evil; who put darkness for light, and light for darkness; who put bitter for sweet, and sweet for bitter!" (Isaiah 5:20).

10. ASHES FROM THE FURNACE: Moses and Aaron used dust from a lime kiln, the type of furnace the Israelite slaves used to make bricks. Here the Lord took the Egyptians' tool of oppression and used it to damage their own health.

11. THE MAGICIANS: Magic and sorcery played a major role in the pantheistic religious system of Egypt. These "magicians" were also called "wise men," as they were the learned "scientists" of their day. They were evidently capable of mimicking some of God's miracles (e.g., Exodus 7:11), but any power they may have possessed came from Satan rather than God.

could not stand before Moses: This is a pun. It is literally true in the sense that the men suffered from boils that prevented them from standing comfortably, and it is also figuratively true: they could not mimic this particular miracle, and they were disgraced.

God Hardens Pharaoh's Heart: *Thus far, Pharaoh had steadfastly refused to humble himself before God. That pattern eventually became unchangeable.*

12. the Lord hardened the heart of Pharaoh: This is the first time that this wording appears. Pharaoh had persistently refused to humble himself and acknowledge the power of God, so eventually the Lord gave him up to his stubbornness. (See Romans 1:28.)

13. Let My people go: Yet even in the midst of Pharaoh's hardened heart, the Lord continued to give him opportunities to repent. We live in the day of God's grace toward mankind, and He is always at work offering people His free gift of salvation. But each time a person refuses, it becomes more difficult to repent.

15. you would have been cut off from the earth: Even in the midst of sending His judgment against Egypt, the Lord was also showing mercy. Had He poured forth the full fury of His wrath, no man or beast would have survived.

16. for this purpose I have raised you up: Pharaoh believed that his authority came directly from his pagan gods because he was one of their descendants, but Moses boldly stood before him and declared that his authority was granted to him only by the Lord. Further, that authority had been given to him, not for his own glory, but in order to bring glory to God—to the very God whom Pharaoh was rejecting and resisting.

19. send now and gather your livestock: Once again we see the mercy and grace of God even in the midst of judgment. He forewarned Pharaoh of what plague was coming next and when it would arrive. He told Pharaoh explicitly what he could do to avoid its devastation, just as He had repeatedly told him that the plagues would stop if he would let His people leave Egypt.

Some Listen, Some Don't: *Pharaoh and his followers finally confess that they have sinned—but only some of them really mean it.*

20–21. He who feared the word of the Lord . . . he who did not: After all the devastation that the Lord had rained down upon Egypt, it seems hard to believe that people would fail to take so simple a precaution to avoid further loss, but this is the nature of man's hardened heart. When a person turns away from God's grace, even common sense cannot soften his heart.

26. IN THE LAND OF GOSHEN: Once again, the Lord sent devastation upon the nation of Egypt, while miraculously preventing any damage at all on His people.

27. I HAVE SINNED THIS TIME: There is a poignant pathos in this comment, as Pharaoh acknowledged that he had sinned—*this time*. He did not acknowledge that he had sinned previously, by stubbornly refusing to release the Israelites, so the Lord knew that he was not truly repentant this time either. As soon as the suffering stopped, he would harden his heart again.

34. HE SINNED YET MORE: As soon as the Lord removed the cause of suffering from Pharaoh, he again became resistant, returning to his former sins. This is not true repentance; it is merely an attempt to avoid suffering. True repentance is demonstrated by "turning away" (the literal meaning of the word) from things that displease the Lord.

∾ FIRST IMPRESSIONS ∾

1. *Why did Pharaoh persistently refuse to release the Israelites?*

2. *Why did the Israelites blame Moses for their suffering? If you had been in their place, how would you have responded?*

3. *In what ways did God show His mercy and grace in the midst of His judgments? What does this reveal about His character?*

4. *Why did God select these specific plagues? What do they reveal about His character? About the Egyptians?*

⌁ SOME KEY PRINCIPLES ⌁

Do not harden your heart against God's Word.

Pharaoh repeatedly refused to obey God's commands to let the Israelites leave Egypt, yet the Lord continued to give him opportunities to repent. Eventually, however, the Lord gave him over to his hardness of heart, allowing him to remain in stubborn rebellion.

The same principle is true today for the lost world around us. We are living in the day of grace, when salvation is freely available to all who believe, but that day will not last forever. The day is coming when the time for repentance will be past. In that dark day, all who have rejected Christ will be cast out of the presence of God for all eternity.

It is a very dangerous matter to resist God's grace. Each time a person refuses to repent, that repentance becomes more difficult. "For He says: 'In an acceptable time I have heard you, and in the day of salvation I have helped you.' Behold, now is the accepted time; behold, now is the day of salvation" (2 Corinthians 6:2).

God uses discipline and suffering to soften our hearts.

The Lord was not being arbitrary when He sent the plagues on Egypt. Each plague was designed to show the Egyptians that there is only one true God and that He is sovereign in the affairs of mankind. He was not pouring out His full wrath upon them; in fact, in each plague He demonstrated mercy and grace. His purpose was not to vent His anger, but to bring the Egyptians to repentance and obedience while simultaneously delivering Israel from their servitude.

The same is true today. The Lord uses hardship to further His purposes in our lives, not to arbitrarily watch us suffer. He uses it to lead people to repentance and salvation, and He uses it in the lives of His people to make us more like His Son, Jesus Christ.

"My brethren, count it all joy when you fall into various trials, knowing that the testing of your faith produces patience. But let patience have its perfect work, that you may be perfect and complete, lacking nothing" (James 1:2–4).

When the world rebels against God's Word, all His people may suffer.

Most of the people of Israel considered themselves innocent bystanders in a struggle between Moses and Pharaoh, and they resented it deeply when they found themselves bearing the brunt of Pharaoh's wrath. But they did not recognize that they were intimately involved in the struggle because it was actually a struggle between Pharaoh and God.

Pharaoh had set himself up in God's place, and he was determined to prove that God had no authority in his life. It was only to be expected, therefore, that he would vent his resentment against the people of God—and all of God's people suffered as a result.

This is often the case, as the New Testament reveals: "If you were of the world, the world would love its own. Yet because you are not of the world, but I chose you out of the world, therefore the world hates you. Remember the word that I said to you, 'A servant is not greater than his master.' If they persecuted Me, they will also persecute you. If they kept My word, they will keep yours also" (John 15:19–20). "Do not marvel, my brethren, if the world hates you" (1 John 3:13). The Israelites' suffering was for a short duration and was nothing compared to the glory that was revealed when they were released from bondage.

⌁ DIGGING DEEPER ⌁

5. *What does it mean that "the LORD hardened the heart of Pharaoh" (Exodus 9:12)? If God hardened Pharaoh's heart, in what way was Pharaoh still responsible for his own actions?*

6. *Why did the Lord permit Pharaoh to persecute His people in the first place? What effect did the persecution have on them?*

7. Pharaoh confessed that he had sinned, yet the Lord sent further plagues. Why? What does it indicate about the sincerity (or lack thereof) of Pharaoh's sorrow?

8. What does it mean to "harden your heart" against God? Give practical examples. Why is this a dangerous practice?

⁀ Taking It Personally ⁀

9. Have you ever hardened your heart toward God? Have you repented of your sins, or merely tried to avoid suffering?

10. When have you seen the Lord using difficult or painful circumstances in your life to bring good? How have you responded during such times of hardship?

~ 3 ~
CROSSING THE RED SEA

EXODUS 14, 16–17

~ HISTORICAL BACKGROUND ~

The people of Israel had just left Egypt, carrying with them great wealth that they had plundered from their former slave masters. They had witnessed unprecedented miracles that the Lord had done on their behalf, and they had seen the Egyptians plagued with great loss while they themselves remained unharmed. God had told them again and again that He planned to carry them out of bondage into the promised land of Canaan, and they had seen that the Lord's promises never fail.

But somehow all of this was quickly forgotten when they faced their very first setback. They had not been traveling for more than a few days when they looked behind them to see Pharaoh's army pursuing them. This was the most powerful army in the world, and it is quite likely that Pharaoh had taken his most elite troops on this expedition. They were equipped with the best weapons of the day, including armed chariots—the equivalent of tanks in our time—and they were well-trained and disciplined fighters. The Israelites, on the other hand, were newly released slaves who had never fought in combat and never wielded weapons. From a human perspective, they were in deep trouble.

Yet the human perspective is just what the Lord wants His people to avoid. He calls us to walk by faith, not by sight—to always be looking to God for assistance rather than to man or to ourselves. God had shown the people of Israel unequivocally that He would fight on their behalf, and He had proven beyond doubt that He would not abandon them. How quickly the people forgot those lessons when they were confronted by the enemy.

We can learn from the forgetfulness of the Israelites, because we are no different from them. It is vital that we remember what the Lord has done in our lives and to expect Him to work on our behalf in the future as He has done in the past.

GOD'S PLAN EXPLAINED: *The Lord tells Moses to lead the people toward the Red Sea, explaining that He has a plan to bring glory to His name in Egypt.*

1. **THE LORD SPOKE TO MOSES:** The Israelites had just left Egypt and were now heading into the desert region.

2. **PI HAHIROTH, BETWEEN MIGDOL AND THE SEA, OPPOSITE BAAL ZEMPHON:** The exact locations of these sites are unknown. See the map in the introduction for various possible routes during this time.

BY THE SEA: That is, the Red Sea.

4. **I WILL HARDEN PHARAOH'S HEART:** As we saw in Study 2, this does not mean that the Lord enticed Pharaoh to do evil. Pharaoh had previously hardened himself against God, and his moments of softening were only temporary; he stubbornly remained set against the God of Israel. The Lord would permit him to revert to his previous attitude toward Israel, using his stubborn wickedness for God's glory.

I WILL GAIN HONOR: Man's wickedness does not frustrate God's plan for His people. He allows men and women to exercise their free will, deciding for themselves whether to submit to Him—but He uses their actions, whether righteous or unrighteous, to bring glory to Himself.

THAT THE EGYPTIANS MAY KNOW THAT I AM THE LORD: God had chosen the descendants of Abraham to be His special people, set apart from the world around them as His special nation. This was not for their personal gain, however; He chose them for the specific purpose of showing forth His glory and mercy to the entire world. He wanted the Egyptians to worship Him just as the Israelites did. He intervened in the affairs of Egypt in order to set His people free from bondage, but also to show Himself to the Egyptians.

ON SECOND THOUGHT: *After the Israelites are gone, the Egyptians wonder why they ever released them in the first place. Pharaoh goes out to bring them back.*

5. **WHY HAVE WE DONE THIS?:** This response is almost humorous in its short-sightedness. The Egyptians had released the Israelites from slavery—indeed, they had *driven* them away—because the Lord's judgments were threatening to destroy their entire land. His final plague had killed the firstborn son of every household! But once life began to settle back to normal, they forgot about the Lord's miraculous interventions and remembered only the huge profit they had enjoyed from the Hebrews' slave labor. This is

a symptom of a heart that is hardened against God, refusing to acknowledge His miraculous displays of power and grace. The religious leaders in Israel would later take the same attitude toward Jesus, denying that His tremendous miracles of healing and raising the dead were displays of God's power—even attributing those miracles to the devil.

8. THE CHILDREN OF ISRAEL WENT OUT WITH BOLDNESS: At this point in their travels, the Israelites were trusting fully in the presence and power of God to protect them. It may have been easy to take such an attitude when the enemy was not close on their heels. Their faith would waver, unfortunately, when Pharaoh's army came into sight.

9. OVERTOOK THEM: Pharaoh's army could travel far more quickly in their chariots than the Israelites could on foot.

PANIC!: *The Israelites are filled with terror when they see Pharaoh's army bearing down on them.*

10. THEY WERE VERY AFRAID: This is quite understandable from a human perspective. Pharaoh's cavalry was the most powerful in the world at the time. It would be comparable to seeing an enemy nation rumbling toward you in tanks and armored vehicles.

CRIED OUT TO THE LORD: This was the proper response for the people to make in this situation. They had seen the Lord's unstoppable power in Egypt, and He had shown them repeatedly that He was their God and that He would not abandon them to their enemies. It would be reasonable to cry out to the Lord to intervene again and then trust Him to do so. Unfortunately, their cry was one of anger, as the next verse reveals.

11. WHY HAVE YOU SO DEALT WITH US? : The Israelites responded to the very first threat in their travels by falsely accusing Moses—and ultimately, God—of treachery. The Lord had performed a great many miracles and wonders in Egypt on their behalf, signs that the whole nation witnessed as demonstrations of God's presence and power. By openly voicing such false accusations against God, the Israelites were declaring to the world around them that they did not trust Him.

12. IT WOULD HAVE BEEN BETTER FOR US TO SERVE THE EGYPTIANS: This would become an almost constant refrain during Israel's travels. This lack of trust in God's faithfulness would eventually prevent this generation from entering the promised land, as we will see in a future study.

13. DO NOT BE AFRAID: The Lord frequently commands His people to take courage. On the one hand, fear is an emotion, and as such is not easily controlled. But on the other hand, we actually breed fear in ourselves and in others by permitting it to take control. We overcome fear by focusing on the promises of God, remembering what He has done for us in the past, and by choosing to place our faith in Him rather than in the circumstances around us. The people had to choose whether to act in fear or in faith.

STAND STILL, AND SEE: In times of crisis, we can actually increase our own fear and anxiety by rushing about, trying to resolve the crisis. There are times when things are beyond our control, and in those times the best response is to be still and see what the Lord will do on our behalf. "Be still, and know that I am God; I will be exalted among the nations, I will be exalted in the earth!" (Psalm 46:10).

14. THE LORD WILL FIGHT FOR YOU: The key to overcoming fear is to deliberately remind ourselves that the all-powerful God is our champion. Hear the words of Paul: "What then shall we say to these things? If God is for us, who can be against us? He who did not spare His own Son, but delivered Him up for us all, how shall He not with Him also freely give us all things?" (Romans 8:31–32).

GOD'S PLAN UNFOLDS: *The Lord tells Moses what to do with the people and then reiterates what He plans to do with the Egyptians. He intends to show everyone that He is God.*

15. GO FORWARD: The Lord had begun a good work in the lives of the Israelites, and He would complete that work regardless of who attempted to prevent it. When people or circumstances conspire against us, our response should still be to "go forward" with the Lord, "being confident of this very thing, that He who has begun a good work in you will complete it until the day of Jesus Christ" (Philippians 1:6).

16. LIFT UP YOUR ROD, AND STRETCH OUT YOUR HAND: The Lord frequently commanded Moses or Aaron to do something prior to His working a great miracle. He did not need Moses' rod to part the Red Sea; there was no magical power in that rod, nor did Moses possess any special powers on his own. The Lord does not even need our obedience to accomplish His purposes; we have already seen that He can achieve His intentions even through the deliberate disobedience and rebellion of men. Nevertheless, He frequently calls us to some act of obedience in order to show the world that His people have faith in Him and that He is faithful and powerful to bring them safely through.

18. THE EGYPTIANS SHALL KNOW THAT I AM THE LORD: The Lord reiterated that His ultimate purpose in this miracle was not to destroy the Egyptians, but to bring glory to His own name and to show the whole world that there is only one true God. It is important to remember, when the Lord works mightily on our behalf, that His purpose is to bring His salvation to all people—even to our enemies.

GOD COMES BETWEEN: *The Lord has been moving before Israel in a pillar of cloud and a pillar of fire. Now He moves the pillar between Israel and Pharaoh's army.*

19. THE ANGEL OF GOD, WHO WENT BEFORE THE CAMP OF ISRAEL: The Lord was present in visible form to His people in a pillar of cloud by day and fire by night, moving in front of the vast horde as they traveled in the wilderness. In this case, however, He moved behind the Israelites in order to protect them.

20. IT CAME BETWEEN THE CAMP OF THE EGYPTIANS AND THE CAMP OF ISRAEL: The Lord intervened visibly between His people and their enemies, showing to both Israel and Egypt that He would not abandon His people.

IT WAS A CLOUD AND DARKNESS TO THE ONE: The Angel of the Lord, and the pillar of cloud and fire, moved from being advance guard (leading the Israelites) to being rear guard (protecting them from danger). The cloud created a blinding barrier between the camps of Israel and Egypt, making it impossible for the Egyptians to continue their pursuit until the cloud was lifted.

21. A STRONG EAST WIND ALL THAT NIGHT: The people did not need to do anything to accomplish their salvation. While they slept, the Lord worked a great miracle in front of them while also protecting them from the enemy behind them.

GOD'S PLAN FULFILLED: *The Lord has miraculously intervened for His people once again, and all that remains is for the people to keep moving forward.*

22. THE CHILDREN OF ISRAEL WENT INTO THE MIDST OF THE SEA: This was an act of faith on the Israelites' part. It must have been daunting to walk between two huge walls of water, especially when they were not held in place by any visible force. The Lord had wrought a powerful miracle to deliver His people, but those people were still required to walk forward in faith. He did not carry them bodily across the Red Sea; their faith and obedience were required if they were to be saved from Pharaoh's army.

23. THE EGYPTIANS PURSUED: This was the ultimate military folly. One would think that Pharaoh would have recognized by now that the power of God was inexorable and that He would not fail to deliver His people. But Pharaoh had willfully blinded himself to the truth by hardening his heart and rejecting the Lord, and he was spiritually incapable of seeing the folly of riding his chariot between two great walls of water that might collapse upon him at any moment.

25. LET US FLEE FROM THE FACE OF ISRAEL: Unfortunately, this realization of God's presence and power came too late for the Egyptians. The day of God's grace does not last forever; those who have steadfastly rejected Him may one day find that they have lost the opportunity to repent.

29. THE CHILDREN OF ISRAEL HAD WALKED ON DRY LAND: The Lord used the same force both to deliver His children and to destroy their enemies.

31. THE PEOPLE FEARED THE LORD, AND BELIEVED THE LORD: When the Lord effects a miracle in our lives, it is important to make an effort to remember that event. The people of Israel would quickly forget the Lord's great deliverance at the Red Sea, even as they had forgotten His great intervention to free them from bondage. Human nature is quick to forget God's faithfulness when circumstances are against us—even if we were praising Him just a day before.

⌒ FIRST IMPRESSIONS ⌒

1. *Why were the Israelites so afraid when they saw Pharaoh's army? How would you have responded in that situation?*

2. *If you had been in the Israelite camp, how would you have felt when the pillar of cloud moved between you and the Egyptians? How well would you have slept that night?*

3. *How do you think the people of Israel felt as they walked through the Red Sea between great walls of water? When they saw Pharaoh's army destroyed?*

4. *Why do you think Pharaoh and his people changed their minds about letting the Israelites go?*

↶ SOME KEY PRINCIPLES ↷

Do not forget what the Lord has done.

The people of Israel had seen many amazing miracles over a short period of time as the Lord demonstrated His power and His determination to set them free from slavery. He had sent ten plagues that devastated Egypt but left the Israelites unharmed. He had spoken to them through Moses, predicting that Pharaoh would drive them out of Egypt, heavily laden with gold and silver—and it had happened exactly as promised. Yet when the first setback occurred, they instantly forgot all those signs and wonders and accused God of betraying them.

This is a characteristic common to all humans—indeed, it is part of our nature. We rejoice when the Lord blesses us, giving Him glory and thanks for His loving intervention in our lives. But then something goes wrong in our lives, some unexpected threat arises—and we are immediately filled with fear and doubt. We wonder if the Lord has abandoned us, or we forget to trust Him and instead try to solve the matter by our own power.

It is vital that we remember what the Lord has done in our lives, so that we don't become fearful when circumstances go against us. If the Lord was faithful in the past, we can be confident that He will be faithful in the future. "Beware that you do not forget the LORD your God by not keeping His commandments, His judgments, and His statutes which I command you today" (Deuteronomy 8:11). "Bless the LORD, O my soul, and forget not all His benefits" (Psalm 103:2).

Do not fear what men may do to you.

Pharaoh was the most powerful man in the most powerful nation on earth. His army was feared around the known world, and they were equipped with the latest technologies and the best training. The Israelites, on the other hand, were newly released slaves with no military experience and no chariots. It is no wonder that they were frightened when they looked behind them and saw the great dust cloud of Pharaoh's army bearing down.

But the greatest army on earth is no match for the power of God. The Lord led them into the Red Sea and then plucked off the wheels of their chariots as simply as a man snaps a toothpick. At the same time, He led His people through the sea, walking on dry ground. They did not even get their feet wet!

Our tendency is to focus on what we can see, to believe the evidence of our senses. But the Lord calls us to walk by faith, not by sight, and to rely fully on His unlimited power and faithfulness. "In God I have put my trust; I will not be afraid. What can man do to me?" (Psalm 56:11). "For He Himself has said, 'I will never leave you nor forsake you.' So we may boldly say: 'The LORD is my helper; I will not fear. What can man do to me?'" (Hebrews 13:5–6).

If we harden our heart, we will become blind to the truth.

Pharaoh stubbornly refused to believe that the Lord was the one true God, and he repeatedly hardened his heart against the Lord's attempts to bring him into submission. Each time Moses warned him that a plague was coming—predicting when it would start, what it would do, and even how its damage could be lessened—yet Pharaoh still would not relent. Even after the Lord had sent horrible devastation on his land, including the death of all firstborn sons, he could not see what should have been painfully obvious: that he could not defeat the power of God.

As mentioned in the previous principle, it is in our human nature to place our faith in the evidence of our senses—but the truth of God cannot always be discerned by our eyes. To discern the truth of God, we must exercise faith, and we must place that faith in the Word of God and in His holy character. When we reject God's Word, however, we willfully blind ourselves to the truth. A person with a hardened heart will walk about like a blind man, stumbling into trouble and falling into pits.

"Oh come, let us worship and bow down; let us kneel before the LORD our Maker. For He is our God, and we are the people of His pasture, and the sheep of His hand. Today, if you will hear His voice: 'Do not harden your hearts, as in the rebellion, as in the day of trial in the wilderness, when your fathers tested Me; they tried Me, though they saw My work'" (Psalm 95:6–9). Today is the day to listen to God's voice.

⌒ DIGGING DEEPER ⌒

5. What were the people implying about God's character when they accused Him of leading them into the wilderness to destroy them?

6. What were the Lord's purposes in doing the miracles of this chapter? What does this teach about His character?

7. Why did the people of Israel accuse God of betraying them? How would you have responded in that situation?

8.   When have you been afraid of what other people could do to you? How did the Lord show His power on your behalf?

↬ Taking It Personally ↫

9.   Have you hardened your heart toward God? What will you do this week to soften your heart?

10. When have you been encouraged by remembering what the Lord has done in your life? When have you become discouraged or afraid because you forgot?

~ 4 ~
THE LAW OF GOD

⌐ HISTORICAL BACKGROUND ¬

The Israelites have left Egypt and traveled into the wilderness toward Mount Sinai. (See the map in the introduction.) It has been exactly three months to the day, and they have camped at the base of Sinai. The Lord has made His presence known with dramatic signs: terrible thunder and lightning, the noise of loud trumpet blasts, and a thick smoke rising up and engulfing the mountain. He has forbidden the people to set foot on the mountain or even to approach it, for He is there and His holiness will not permit the presence of sin.

The people are filled with fear, for they recognize that they are in the presence of a holy God, and it convicts them of their sinful state. What hope do they have of ever knowing God? Yet God invites Moses up onto the mountain, and He gives him a series of commandments by which the people are to live. Through His Law, God's people are given a means of access into His presence—a very distant and incomplete access, but a means of knowing God all the same.

The entire Law is detailed and long, too long for a single study such as this. But on this occasion the Lord gave Moses a sort of summary, ten commandments that encapsulate the entire law. These commandments teach us today, just as they taught the Israelites, what it means in practical terms to follow God's moral law. Jesus and the New Testament writers refer back to the Ten Commandments frequently, as we will see in this study. In fact, Jesus summarized all of the law with the two greatest commandments: love God with all your heart, and love your neighbor as yourself.

⌐ READING EXODUS 20:1–21 ¬

GOD SPEAKS: *Just three months after the Israelites leave Egypt, Moses ascends Mount Sinai. There, the Lord gives him the Ten Commandments.*

1. GOD SPOKE: The Israelites were encamped near the base of Mount Sinai, and the Lord had called Moses to ascend the mountain so that He could speak to him. These teachings are known as the Ten Commandments. The Law God gave to Moses was far more detailed, listing many different sacrifices and worship practices, as well as specifics on forbidden actions and their consequences. The Ten Commandments, though, briefly summarize what the Lord expects of His people, who are called to be holy and set apart from the world around them.

2. I AM THE LORD: The word translated "Lord" in the Old Testament (often printed in all capitals, as in the New King James Version) is *Jehovah*, meaning "the existing one." The name is also sometimes spelled *Yahweh*.

IDOLATRY: *The Lord's first commandment is the most detailed. God's people are to worship Him, and Him alone.*

3. NO OTHER GODS BEFORE ME: This does not mean that God's people are permitted to have other gods, so long as they are of less importance than the Lord. It literally means "you shall have no other gods *in My face*, no other gods in my presence." In short, God's people are to worship and serve Him alone, and we are to take care not to allow anything else to become a false god in our lives.

4. CARVED IMAGE: The people of Moses' day frequently made statues of animals or mythical gods that they prayed to and worshipped. The Israelites themselves would soon make a golden calf, even as Moses was on the mountain speaking with God! It is in our sinful human nature to desire a god that can be seen and handled, but the Lord calls His people to walk by faith rather than by sight.

5. BOW DOWN TO THEM NOR SERVE THEM: Bowing before something indicates that a person is submitting himself to that idol's authority. Serving involves labor, using the work of one's hands to please an idol or to further an idol's goals. Many things can become idols in a person's life, not just carved images of bulls or fish. We risk making anything an idol when we give it authority in our lives, allowing something to determine our daily schedule or making it a top financial priority.

A JEALOUS GOD: This sense of jealousy is akin to the protective jealousy that a man has toward his wife, resenting any attempt to woo her away from him. The Lord is passionately protective of His people, and His anger burns toward anyone or anything that tries to draw away their worship.

VISITING THE INIQUITY OF THE FATHERS UPON THE CHILDREN: This does not mean that children are punished for their parents' sins, which, in fact, is forbidden according to God's Law (Deuteronomy 24:16). It means that the sin of idolatry will affect a person's children for several generations. A man who worships something besides the one true God will pass on that idolatry to his children, and God's judgment will also last for several generations.

THOSE WHO HATE ME: The Lord made a black-and-white distinction here: anyone who does not worship Him hates Him; anyone who allows an idol to take precedence in his life hates God. "No one can serve two masters," Jesus later confirmed, "for either he will hate the one and love the other, or else he will be loyal to the one and despise the other. You cannot serve God and mammon" (Matthew 6:24).

6. THOUSANDS: God's judgment would fall upon idolaters to the third and fourth generation, but His mercy would be lavished upon thousands. This underscores that God's mercy is far greater and far more frequent than His wrath.

SWEARING AND SABBATH: *The Lord warns against taking false oaths, which brings discredit to His name. He also reminds His people to rest on the seventh day.*

7. TAKE THE NAME OF THE LORD YOUR GOD IN VAIN: The Lord had revealed His name to Moses on several occasions, and in our last study He revealed His glory. These gifts, however, also bring responsibility to God's people. We are permitted to know His name, but we are equally forbidden to abuse that name. Such abuse includes anything that will bring disrepute on His character, such as making false claims or promises. "You have heard that it was said to those of old, 'You shall not swear falsely, but shall perform your oaths to the Lord.' But I say to you, do not swear at all: . . . But let your 'Yes' be 'Yes,' and your 'No,' 'No.' For whatever is more than these is from the evil one" (Matthew 5:33, 34, 37).

8–11. REMEMBER THE SABBATH DAY: The Lord created the entire universe, including mankind, in six literal twenty-four-hour days, and He rested on the seventh day. He then "blessed the Sabbath day and hallowed it," meaning that the Lord added a special blessing into His laws of creation for those who followed His example by resting on the seventh day. However, Jesus later warned against legalistic observation of the Law, including the Sabbath laws. "The Sabbath was made for man, and not man for the Sabbath" (Mark 2:27). Significantly, the command to observe the Sabbath is not repeated in the New Testament, whereas the other nine of the Ten Commandments are. In fact, it is clearly nullified (see Colossians 2:16, 17), meaning it is no longer binding for God's people. Because it was specifically intended for Israel under the Mosaic economy, the Sabbath mandate does not directly apply to believers today (who are part of the church age).

HONOR YOUR PARENTS: *This is the first command that brings with it a positive promise. Honor your parents, and you will live a long life.*

12. HONOR YOUR FATHER AND YOUR MOTHER: To "honor" means to esteem highly, to respect. It includes the elements of obeying our parents when we are young and caring for them when they are old.

THAT YOUR DAYS MAY BE LONG: In the New Testament, Paul echoed this very teaching of the Law, quoting from the book of Deuteronomy: "Children, obey your parents in the Lord, for this is right. 'Honor your father and mother,' which is the first commandment with promise: 'that it may be well with you and you may live long on the earth'" (Ephesians 6:1–3).

GETTING ALONG WITH OTHERS: *The following commandments teach us how to live in peace with our neighbors.*

13. MURDER: Jesus would later remind His people of this law and would teach them that undue anger is no better: "You have heard that it was said to those of old, 'You shall not murder, and whoever murders will be in danger of the judgment.' But I say to you that whoever is angry with his brother without a cause shall be in danger of the judgment" (Matthew 5:21–22). Later, the apostle John wrote, "Whoever hates his brother is a murderer, and you know that no murderer has eternal life abiding in him" (1 John 3:15).

14. ADULTERY: Again, Jesus took this commandment seriously and taught that lust in the heart was equal to adultery in the body (in terms of its culpability before God): "You have heard that it was said to those of old, 'You shall not commit adultery.' But I say to you that whoever looks at a woman to lust for her has already committed adultery with her in his heart" (Matthew 5:27–28).

15. STEAL: Nothing changed with regard to theft between the old covenant and the new. "Let him who stole steal no longer," Paul wrote, "but rather let him labor, working with his hands what is good, that he may have something to give him who has need" (Ephesians 4:28).

16. FALSE WITNESS: Jesus taught that the penchant to lie against one's neighbor comes straight from man's heart—and defiles him: "But those things which proceed out of the mouth come from the heart, and they defile a man. For out of the heart proceed evil thoughts, murders, adulteries, fornications, thefts, false witness, blasphemies" (Matthew 15:18–19).

17. COVET: "Where do wars and fights come from among you?" wrote James, the brother of Christ. "Do they not come from your desires for pleasure that war in your members? You lust and do not have. You murder and covet and cannot obtain. You fight and war. Yet you do not have because you do not ask. You ask and do not receive, because you ask amiss, that you may spend it on your pleasures" (James 4:1–3). Coveting gets you nowhere.

GOD'S TERRIFYING PRESENCE: *The Lord reminds His people that they should not take lightly their privilege of entering His presence.*

18. THUNDERINGS: See Exodus 19:16. The Lord made His presence known in very powerful symbols, both audible and visible. The people witnessed terrific thunderclaps, lightning flashes, terrifying trumpet blasts, and a thick smoke engulfing the top of Mount Sinai. The presence of God is a frightening thing to sinful men and women. Christians can enter His presence boldly and with confidence only because we are covered by the blood of the Lamb, His Son Jesus Christ. Without Christ, God's presence would be terrible and deadly.

19. LET NOT GOD SPEAK WITH US, LEST WE DIE: This was not because the Lord was angry with the people, but simply because He was holy and they were not. Again, the Christian's access to the Father is made possible only by the propitiation of His Son. Prior to Christ, no man but the high priest could enter His presence and live, and that occurred only once a year according to rigorous stipulations.

20. SO THAT YOU MAY NOT SIN: It is very purifying to be reminded of the awe-inspiring holiness and power of God. It can be easy for Christians to take God's goodness for granted, indulging in sinful behavior and expecting a "cheap grace." But Paul the apostle warned about this very inclination: "What shall we say then? Shall we continue in sin that grace may abound? Certainly not! How shall we who died to sin live any longer in it?" (Romans 6:1–2).

✥ FIRST IMPRESSIONS ✥

1. *Review the Ten Commandments and put each into your own words. Give practical examples of each from your own life.*

2. What does it mean to honor one's parents, in practical terms? How is this done as an adult?

3. What does it mean to covet? Give practical examples from modern life.

4. Why did Jesus say that lusting after another person is the same as committing adultery? Or that hating another person is the same as committing murder in your heart? What implications does such teaching regarding heart attitudes hold for your life?

ᑐ Some Key Principles ᑕ

Living by the Ten Commandments will not bring eternal life.

The Lord gave His people the Law in order to show them what He expects of His children and to provide a temporary measure of sacrifice for sins. But the Law could not save anyone, because animal sacrifices and behavioral rules cannot change the heart or make final atonement for sin. Only the blood of Christ, God's perfect sacrificial Lamb, can provide forgiveness for man's sin and reconciliation with a holy God.

Paul taught that the Law was given to God's people in order to make them fully aware of their sinful state, to demonstrate that it was impossible to enter the presence of a holy God simply because man could never be holy in himself. Sin is a part of our nature that cannot be erased by good deeds. In fact, it is impossible for fallen men and women to keep God's law perfectly.

"For we know that the law is spiritual, but I am carnal, sold under sin. For what I am doing, I do not understand. For what I will to do, that I do not practice; but what I hate, that I do. If, then, I do what I will not to do, I agree with the law that it is good. But now, it is no longer I who do it, but sin that dwells in me. For I know that in me (that is, in my flesh) nothing good dwells; for to will is present with me, but how to perform what is good I do not find. For the good that I will to do, I do not do; but the evil I will not to do, that I practice. Now if I do what I will not to do, it is no longer I who do it, but sin that dwells in me. I find then a law, that evil is present with me, the one who wills to do good. For I delight in the law of God according to the inward man. But I see another law in my members, warring against the law of my mind, and bringing me into captivity to the law of sin which is in my members. O wretched man that I am! Who will deliver me from this body of death? I thank God—through Jesus Christ our Lord!" (Romans 7:14–25).

The Ten Commandments are still valid for Christians today.

God gave the Law as a temporary measure to enable God's people to enter His presence and live in obedience to His will. The death and resurrection of Christ were the final atonement for sin, and it is only through faith in Christ that anyone can find peace with God. Nevertheless, the Ten Commandments (with the exception of the Sabbath) still present principles of godliness that God expects of His people today.

The many New Testament passages we have just quoted demonstrate this. Jesus came to fulfill the Law by providing free access into the presence of God through His final sacrifice, and He gave us His Holy Spirit to enable us to fulfill the principles of godliness—the principles outlined in the Ten Commandments—in our own lives. Those principles of godly behavior are as important today as they were in Moses' day.

"Do not think that I came to destroy the Law or the Prophets," Christ Himself said. "I did not come to destroy but to fulfill. For assuredly, I say to you, till heaven and earth pass away, one jot or one tittle will by no means pass from the law till all is fulfilled. Whoever therefore breaks one of the least of these commandments, and teaches men so, shall be called least in the kingdom of heaven; but whoever does and teaches them, he shall be called great in the kingdom of heaven" (Matthew 5:17–19).

All of God's Law is summarized by the two greatest commandments.

A young man asked Jesus, "Teacher, which is the great commandment in the law?" Jesus answered him, "'You shall love the Lord your God with all your heart, with all your soul, and with all your mind.' This is the first and great commandment. And the second is like it:'You shall love your neighbor as yourself.' On these two commandments hang all the Law and the Prophets" (Matthew 22:36–40).

The Ten Commandments themselves fall into these two categories. Some of them spell out what it means to love God with all our hearts, souls, and minds, while others give practical ways of loving our neighbors as ourselves. Together, these two principles summarize what it means to live a godly life.

"For the commandments, 'You shall not commit adultery,' 'You shall not murder,' 'You shall not steal,' 'You shall not bear false witness,' 'You shall not covet,' and if there is any other commandment, are all summed up in this saying, namely, 'You shall love your neighbor as yourself.' Love does no harm to a neighbor; therefore love is the fulfillment of the law" (Romans 13:9–10).

↳ DIGGING DEEPER ↲

5. *Review the Ten Commandments, dividing them into these two categories:*

Love God with all your heart

6. Which of the commandments do you struggle to obey? Which do you find fairly easy?

7. What does it mean to "love the Lord your God with all your heart, with all your soul, and with all your mind" (Matthew 22:37)? What is involved in this?

8.   What does it mean to love your neighbor as yourself? How does this compare with our culture's emphasis on self-esteem and self-fulfillment?

⌁ Taking It Personally ⌁

9.   Which of the Ten Commandments convicts you of sin? How might the Lord be leading you to change this week?

10. Are you living by the two greatest commandments? How can you deepen your love of God? Your love for others?

MOSES ON THE MOUNTAIN

EXODUS 33–34

⌐ HISTORICAL BACKGROUND ⌐

The Lord has now led His people out of Egypt, and they have seen His power and glory throughout their trip. Pharaoh pursued them as they left Egypt, and they found themselves trapped by the Red Sea—only to see God part the sea and allow them to cross on dry land, while drowning their enemies behind them. The Lord has been traveling with them in the desert, going before them and behind them in a pillar of cloud by day and fire by night. He has revealed to them many things about His character and what He expects of His people, and He has begun to outline His law through Moses.

The Lord has also given the people detailed instructions concerning a portable tabernacle, which they will carry throughout their wilderness wanderings. The tabernacle contains an open courtyard, surrounded by curtains, that the people of Israel are permitted to enter. Within that courtyard, however, is a smaller tent, divided in two. The outer portion of that tent is the Holy Place, and only priests are permitted to enter it. Within the Holy Place is the Most Holy Place, where the ark of the covenant is kept—and only the high priest is permitted to enter this area once a year. This is the area in which the Lord symbolically resides among His people, and anyone other than the High Priest who enters His presence will be struck dead.

All of these details accentuate the fact that mankind could not approach God. Mankind is sinful, and God is holy—He will not permit a sinner to enter His presence, and no one can look upon His face and survive. Yet in spite of this terrible gulf of separation, God still remained present with His people as they left Egypt. He was present in the pillars of cloud and fire; He was present in His tabernacle; and He was present with Moses on Mount Sinai. God even spoke with Moses "face to face," as one friend speaks to another. This was the relationship Moses had as he spoke with God on Mount Sinai, and it was similar to the intimate relationship Christians freely enjoy today with God through the blood of Jesus Christ.

⌒ READING EXODUS 33:9–23 ⌒

SPEAKING WITH GOD: *The Lord's presence traveled with the Israelites in a pillar of cloud or fire, and Moses spoke with Him face to face.*

9. THE TABERNACLE: The Lord had given the Israelites specific instructions on how to make a portable tabernacle for their use during the exodus from Egypt. (See Exodus 25.)

THE PILLAR OF CLOUD: The Angel of the Lord traveled with God's people during their exodus and wilderness wanderings in a pillar of cloud during the day and a pillar of fire at night. The cloud shielded the people from the sun, while the fire provided light in the darkness. Each provided a visible manifestation of the Lord to guide the people and remind them of His presence.

11. FACE TO FACE: The Lord did not literally show His face to Moses, as we will see in this chapter. Nevertheless, He spoke with Moses intimately and audibly, as two men might speak together in private.

AS A MAN SPEAKS TO HIS FRIEND: Abraham was called "a friend of God" (James 2:23), and Moses, too, shared an intimacy with the Lord that is enjoyed by close friends. Christians are also called God's friends: "You are My friends if you do whatever I command you. No longer do I call you servants, for a servant does not know what his master is doing; but I have called you friends, for all things that I heard from My Father I have made known to you" (John 15:14–15).

12. I KNOW YOU BY NAME: God's friendship is no mere acquaintance—He knows His people intimately. "The very hairs of your head are all numbered" (Luke 12:7).

A GODLY LEADER: *Moses demonstrates several important aspects of godly leadership as he interacts with the Lord.*

SHOW ME NOW YOUR WAY: The Lord had called Moses to lead a vast horde of God's people on a trek through the wilderness to the promised land, but Moses recognized his own limitations. He felt inadequate for the task and asked the Lord to give him wisdom and knowledge—wisdom to lead and knowledge of God's character. This is the mark of a godly leader, recognizing that one's strength is insufficient and relying on God for wisdom and knowledge.

CONSIDER THAT THIS NATION IS YOUR PEOPLE: Moses interceded regularly for the people under his leadership. On several occasions, the Lord's anger burned against the people, but Moses interceded on their behalf, and the Lord stayed His hand of judgment. This is another mark of a godly leader, praying regularly for those under his authority.

16. HOW THEN WILL IT BE KNOWN: Moses also was concerned about the people's witness to the world around them. If the Lord's presence was not obvious to the world, Moses reasoned, then His people would not be any different from the world. This, too, is a mark of a godly leader, to be jealous of the Lord's reputation, ensuring that one's own life and ministry are bearing a good witness of the Lord's presence.

SHOW ME YOUR GLORY: *Moses makes an amazingly bold request of the Lord, asking to see His glory. But no man may see God's face and live.*

18. SHOW ME YOUR GLORY: This is actually an incredibly bold request. The Lord had already revealed His glory to some extent in the pillars of cloud and fire, and He had made known His unlimited power by plagues and miracles from Egypt onward. He met with Moses regularly and spoke to him as a friend—and yet Moses wanted more! What is perhaps even more amazing is the fact that God was not displeased with the request. The Lord actually wants His children to hunger for deeper intimacy with Him, yearning to know Him more truly and profoundly than we already do.

19. ALL MY GOODNESS: The Lord revealed His character to Moses, showing him still more of His goodness, mercy, justice, and grace. This is a mystery; we are not told specifically what Moses saw, nor can we conceive how the full goodness of God could be perceived by human eyes.

THE NAME OF THE LORD: As we have seen previously, a person's name was thought to embody his character, to describe his true nature. The name of the Lord is the expression of His nature, encapsulating who He is—"I AM WHO I AM" (Exodus 3:14).

I WILL BE GRACIOUS TO WHOM I WILL BE GRACIOUS: This does not mean that the Lord is capricious, showing grace in an arbitrary manner. Rather, it means that He is absolutely sovereign, and He orders the affairs of mankind as He sees fit. If He chooses to bestow His grace upon a person, nothing can prevent it.

20. YOU CANNOT SEE MY FACE: Sinful man cannot enter the holy presence of God. Adam once walked with God, speaking to Him face to face, but after he sinned, he was cast out of God's presence. Through the blood of Christ, however, our fellowship with God is restored, "for through Him we . . . have access by one Spirit to the Father" (Ephesians 2:18). In eternity, God's people shall see Him face to face.

22. I WILL PUT YOU IN THE CLEFT OF THE ROCK: Moses was enabled to see some of God's glory because he was protected in the "cleft of the rock." In the same way, Christians are enabled to see God's face because we are protected by the Rock of Ages, bathed in the blood of Jesus Christ.

ᕐ READING EXODUS 34:29–35 ᕐ

MOSES WEARS A VEIL: *Moses goes up Mount Sinai to receive the Ten Commandments from the Lord, and his face glows with God's reflected glory.*

29. MOUNT SINAI: See the map in the introduction. Mount Sinai was the place where the Lord met with Moses and gave him the Ten Commandments. We will return to this in Study 4.

THE TWO TABLETS OF THE TESTIMONY: The Ten Commandments. These were the second set of stone tablets, as Moses had smashed the first set in anger upon discovering that the Israelites were worshiping a golden calf. (See Exodus 32.)

THE SKIN OF HIS FACE SHONE: Moses' face glowed with a reflection of God's glory because he had been in the presence of the Lord, speaking to him "face to face." Similarly, the people with whom we interact can discern when we have been in the presence of the Lord (as they see the fruit of His Spirit displayed in our actions and attitudes). (See 2 Corinthians 3:7–17.)

30. THEY WERE AFRAID TO COME NEAR HIM: The holiness of God is so unapproachable to sinful men that even a mere reflection of it is terrifying. Jesus called His followers to be light in a world of darkness, reflecting His own light—for we are "the light of the world" (Matthew 5:14). It can be both compelling and frightening when others see the light of Christ's holiness reflected in our lives.

33. HE PUT A VEIL ON HIS FACE: The Holiest of Holies within the tabernacle was the place where the high priest met with God annually. The ark of the covenant, representing the presence of God, was kept there. This section was separated from the rest of the tabernacle by a heavy veil to prevent anyone from entering the presence of God—for to do so meant certain death. But when Jesus died on the cross, that veil was miraculously torn apart from top to bottom, indicating that Christians now have access directly to the Father through the death of Christ. Paul wrote that though "the children of Israel could not look steadily at the face of Moses because of the glory of his countenance," that reflection of God's glory "was passing away" (2 Corinthians 3:7). The shining countenance was a mere reflection of God's glory, not of any glory within Moses himself, and it faded when he was not in the presence of the Lord. Though our faces do not literally glow, the glory of God is also reflected through the lives of His children today. And because we have the Holy Spirit Himself dwelling within us, that reflection does not fade away.

~ First Impressions ~

1. *List some of the ways that God showed His glory to the people of Israel. What did these things reveal about His character?*

2. *What is meant by "God's glory"? When have you seen some of God's glory in your own life?*

3. *Why were the people afraid of Moses' glowing face? Why did he need a veil?*

4. *Whom do you know that reflects the glory of God in his or her life? What aspect of His glory is reflected? What about in your life?*

⌁ Some Key Principles ⌁

The Lord wants His children to draw closer to Him.

Moses made an audacious request of God when he asked to see His glory. After all, the Lord was already showing His presence among His people in many astonishing ways, including miracles and power and glory. Yet Moses yearned to know more about God, and the Lord was pleased to grant him as much as he was able to bear.

In the same way, the Lord has already revealed much of His glory to His people today by redeeming us from sin and making His presence freely available to all Christians. Yet there is so much more to know! We can deepen our understanding of His character through diligently reading and studying the Bible and by humbly asking Him to teach us more about Himself. "Draw near to God and He will draw near to you" (James 4:8).

We were once separated from God's presence, but Christ has given us free access.

Moses veiled his face because the Israelites could not bear to look upon the glow of God's glory—even though it was just a fading reflection. The Israelites were God's chosen people, yet even they were not permitted into the presence of God within the tabernacle, but were cut off by a thick veil. God had to keep His presence veiled from the people, because they could not look upon His glory and survive.

But when Jesus died on the cross, the veil in the temple was torn asunder (Matthew 27:51)—ripped from the top to the bottom, suggesting that God Himself had eagerly torn the veil away from His presence. God was making it plain to His people that He would no longer remove Himself from them, that His children would henceforth have free access into His presence.

The writer of Hebrews wrote, "Therefore, brethren, having boldness to enter the Holiest by the blood of Jesus, by a new and living way which He consecrated for us, through the veil, that is, His flesh, and having a High Priest over the house of God, let us draw near with a true heart in full assurance of faith, having our hearts sprinkled from an evil conscience and our bodies washed with pure water" (10:19–22).

We reflect God's glory to the world around us—if we first draw close to Him.

Moses spent time on Mount Sinai in communion with the Lord, and when he returned to the camp, his face was glowing brilliantly with a reflection of God's glory. He was unaware of it, but the people were so startled that they were afraid to come near him. God's glory rested on him to such a degree that his presence was nearly as frightening to them as the presence of God Himself—so much so that he had to cover his face with a veil.

That glow faded, however, as Moses spent time away from God's presence. It was only the time that he spent on Sinai that "recharged" the glory to his countenance, for it was actually a reflection of God's glory rather than some holiness or power within himself. In the same way, Christians reflect the character of God as we spend time in His presence. The people with whom we interact on a daily basis can see the character of God reflected in our lives through our actions and attitudes, even when we are sometimes unaware of it ourselves.

But that outward "glow" can fade when we fail to spend time in His presence. It is important, therefore, that God's people spend time with God on a regular basis. Personal Bible reading and prayer, collective worship, and sound biblical teaching are all ways that we deepen our fellowship with God and our fervor for His glory.

⌁ DIGGING DEEPER ⌁

5. How did Moses demonstrate the qualities of godly leadership? How can you imitate him in your own areas of leadership?

6. Why did Moses ask to see God's glory? If you had been in his place, what would you have asked?

7. Why is it that no man can see the face of God and live? What does this reveal about God's glory? About man's sinful condition?

8. How do you draw into God's presence? What can you do to deepen your understanding of His character?

ᕦ Taking It Personally ᕤ

9. Are you a friend of God? What can you do to deepen that friendship?

10. How much of God's glory do people see in your life? What might be veiling that glory from their view?

Section 2:

Characters

In This Section:

~ 6 ~

MOSES

EXODUS 17, NUMBERS 20, HEBREWS 11

✦ CHARACTER'S BACKGROUND ✦

Moses was a very humble man (Numbers 12:3), a man whose life was characterized by faithful obedience to God. He had been miraculously kept alive when Pharaoh ordered the death of all Hebrew male children, and the Lord had worked events so that he was brought up by Pharaoh's daughter. He enjoyed the best that Egypt offered, and he faced a lifetime of security and influence. Yet he abandoned all that in order to be identified with God's people, who were the lowest of slaves.

Moses obeyed God's call to lead the people out of bondage, despite the fact that he felt completely inadequate and unprepared. He spent the rest of his life interceding for the Israelites, acting as an intermediary between them and God, and demonstrating in his own life what it meant to obey the Lord. He did this, furthermore, in the face of constant rebellion and complaining from the people, and he remained humbly obedient to God even when the Israelites said that he was unworthy to lead them.

But even such a great man as Moses was still a sinner, and he was capable of failure in his walk with God. On one notable occasion, he lost his temper and failed to follow God's exact command when the people needed water. From a human perspective, it was a very small lapse, easily excused by the pressures he was under. But his disobedience was very significant in God's eyes, and it resulted in his not entering the promised land.

Nevertheless, Moses is listed in Hebrews 11 as one of the great heroes of our faith, and his life provides us with an excellent example of walking in obedience.

✦ READING EXODUS 17:1–7 ✦

NO WATER TO DRINK: *The people of Israel have been in the desert for one month— and suddenly there is no water.*

1. **WILDERNESS OF SIN:** The exact location of this desert is uncertain, but it was probably not far from Mount Sinai. The name "Sin" is from "Sinai," not related to the English word *sin*.

THERE WAS NO WATER FOR THE PEOPLE TO DRINK: The Lord had promised to lead His people out of Egypt and into Canaan, but He had not promised that their trip would be without some hardships. Nevertheless, each hardship provided the Lord an opportunity to show forth His power and grace to the people as He miraculously solved the problem. He had done this when the Egyptian army pursued them; He had removed the insurmountable obstacle of the Red Sea. Finding water in the desert was easy by comparison.

BLAMING GOD: *The people respond to their circumstances by fighting against Moses, and they falsely accuse God of betraying them.*

2. THE PEOPLE CONTENDED WITH MOSES: Once again we find the people of Israel contending with Moses during a time of hardship rather than turning to the Lord and expecting Him to solve the problem.

WHY DO YOU TEMPT THE LORD? : That is, "Why are you putting the Lord to the test?" The Lord was actually testing, or proving, the faith of the people by allowing them to face some deprivation for a time to see whether they would trust Him to meet their needs. Instead of rising to the occasion and passing the test, however, the people tried to turn the tables and test the Lord's patience.

3. TO KILL US AND OUR CHILDREN: Once again, the people falsely accused Moses and the Lord. They knew that the Lord fully intended to take them safely into Canaan, and they had seen repeatedly that He was faithful to do as He promised. But instead of trusting Him to care for them as He had in the past, they accused Him of intending to betray them.

4. WHAT SHALL I DO WITH THIS PEOPLE?: Moses was just a normal man, made of the same flesh and blood as we are and subject to the same frustrations and weariness that we all know. The people of Israel frequently contended with him as they were doing here, blaming him for their temporary misfortunes and accusing him of treachery. On more than one occasion, the people even rose up to reject him as their leader. In this passage, we get a small glimpse of the exasperation he must have felt as he gave his all for the people, only to receive anger in return.

THEY ARE ALMOST READY TO STONE ME!: This demonstrates the degree of rebellion that was already growing in the hearts of the people. (We will look at this further in Study 11.) When they rejected Moses as their leader, they were effectively rejecting Jehovah as their Lord.

STRIKE THE ROCK: *The Lord has Moses strike a rock, which brings forth abundant water. This also presents us with a picture of Christ.*

6. I WILL STAND BEFORE YOU THERE ON THE ROCK: The Lord would make His presence conspicuous to the people, as He had been doing through the pillars of cloud and fire, so there could be no doubt that it was He who provided water miraculously. Later, the apostle Paul would allude to this passage in describing "that spiritual Rock" from whom living water is provided to God's people today: "Moreover, brethren, I do not want you to be unaware that all our fathers were under the cloud, all passed through the sea, all were baptized into Moses in the cloud and in the sea, all ate the same spiritual food, and all drank the same spiritual drink. For they drank of that spiritual Rock that followed them, and that Rock was Christ" (1 Corinthians 10:1–4).

YOU SHALL STRIKE THE ROCK: The Lord commanded Moses to strike the rock with his staff, prefiguring the day when God Himself would strike His Son, who is the Rock of our salvation. Water flowed from the smitten rock to sustain the lives of God's people, just as Christ's death brings redemption and eternal life to those who trust in Him.

7. MASSAH AND MERIBAH: Meaning "testing" and "contending."

✍ READING NUMBERS 20:1–13 ✍

NO WATER, PART 2: *The Israelites have now been wandering in the wilderness for many years, and they find themselves without water once again. Their response has not changed.*

1. WILDERNESS OF ZIN: See the map in the Introduction. The events of this section took place after the Israelites had been wandering in the wilderness for many years.

MIRIAM: Moses' sister.

2. THERE WAS NO WATER: Once again, the people were faced with the identical test they had faced once before. But rather than learn from that experience to trust the Lord, they reacted in the same way as before, rebelling against Moses and against the Lord.

3. WHEN OUR BRETHREN DIED: Korah had led the people to rise up against Moses and reject him as their leader. The Lord had caused the earth to open and swallow up Korah and his family, and more than 250 people were consumed in a divine fire. The next day, more people came to Moses and accused him of slaughtering Korah and his followers— so the Lord sent a devastating plague that wiped out more than 14,000 Israelites. (See

Numbers 16.) The people were now saying something truly dreadful when they wished that they had been among those slain with Korah, for the Lord made it clear that those people were accursed.

4. THAT WE AND OUR ANIMALS SHOULD DIE HERE: Once again, the people were falsely accusing God and Moses of planning to betray them—despite the fact that the Lord had miraculously sustained them for many years in their wilderness wanderings.

5. TO BRING US TO THIS EVIL PLACE: The Israelites' complaints were really quite astounding in their audacity. They had been slaves in Egypt, treated with disdain and forced to make bricks without straw. The Lord was leading them to the promised land, a land flowing with milk and honey, and He had been abundantly faithful and gracious to them for many years. Yet they dared to suggest that the Lord's promised land was an evil place and that the Egypt of their slavery was better.

SPEAK TO THE ROCK: *The Lord resolves the problem this time just as He had years earlier, except that this time Moses is not to strike the rock, but to speak to it instead.*

---

6. THEY FELL ON THEIR FACES: Moses' life was characterized by prayer. He was continually frustrated by the stubbornness and rebellion of the people, and he always responded by throwing himself before the Lord for guidance and strength. On this particular day, however, Moses would allow his temper to flare up.

8. SPEAK TO THE ROCK: The Lord had miraculously made water flow from a rock years prior to this event when He had directed Moses to strike the rock with his staff. This time, however, Moses was to speak to the rock rather than strike it.

10. MUST WE BRING WATER: Moses, in his exasperation and weariness, forgot that it was not his power that worked so many miracles in the past. His life had always been distinguished by meekness, and he never took the glory to himself for the Lord's deeds, but on this occasion he lost sight of that fact, and the consequences were severe.

11. MOSES LIFTED HIS HAND AND STRUCK THE ROCK: From a human perspective, this seems like a small error, but the Lord's word should never be treated lightly.

12. TO HALLOW ME IN THE EYES OF THE CHILDREN OF ISRAEL: Moses disobeyed the command of the Lord, and by doing so he demonstrated to the people that the Lord was not worthy of his obedience. He did not treat the Lord as holy.

YOU SHALL NOT BRING THIS ASSEMBLY INTO THE LAND: Moses' disobedience was motivated by the same rebellious spirit that had motivated Korah and his followers years earlier (Numbers 27:14), and for this the Lord would not allow him to enter the promised land.

⤜ READING HEBREWS 11:24–29 ⤛

HERO OF THE FAITH: *Despite Moses' sin, he is still listed in the New Testament as a great hero of the faith.*

24. BY FAITH MOSES: Despite Moses' action in striking the rock, he was a model of faith, and he is thus listed in the "faith hall of fame" in Hebrews 11.

REFUSED TO BE CALLED THE SON OF PHARAOH'S DAUGHTER: Moses had been brought up by Pharaoh's daughter and was treated like one of Pharaoh's family. He was in a position of high power and prestige and could easily have remained there for the rest of his life. But he chose instead to identify with the Hebrews, the lowest class of slaves in Egypt. He never forgot that he was a Hebrew by birth and that the Lord had miraculously saved him from Pharaoh's decree of death to Hebrew males.

25. TO SUFFER AFFLICTION WITH THE PEOPLE OF GOD: Moses endured the same hardships that the Israelites experienced during their wilderness wanderings. What is equally pertinent is that he suffered affliction from the people themselves, enduring their continual grumbling and rebellion while remaining faithful to God's commands.

ENJOY THE PASSING PLEASURES OF SIN: It is not sinful to enjoy legitimate pleasure in life, but it is sinful to lose sight of the fact that this world's enjoyments are very temporary and will soon pass away. Moses gave up the many pleasures and privileges of his royal situation in Egypt because he knew that the things of God are eternal. He had his eyes fixed on God's kingdom, not on man's kingdom.

26. ESTEEMING THE REPROACH OF CHRIST: Moses suffered reproach for the sake of Christ in the sense that he identified himself with the Lord's people in their suffering rather than with the household of Pharaoh. He also identified himself with Christ in his role as leader and prophet (Deuteronomy 18:15). Anyone who suffers for his or her faith in God or for the gospel suffers for the sake of Christ.

FOR HE LOOKED TO THE REWARD: Moses had his eyes always fixed upon the things of eternity, ignoring the present world and its allurements, "for he waited for the city which has foundations, whose builder and maker is God" (Hebrews 11:10).

27. HE ENDURED AS SEEING HIM WHO IS INVISIBLE: Moses' faith was such that he responded to God's commands as though God were standing visibly before him. This was the basis for his loyalty to God, and it should be a believer's example as well: "For our light affliction, which is but for a moment, is working for us a far more exceeding and eternal weight of glory, while we do not look at the things which are seen, but at the things which are not seen. For the things which are seen are temporary, but the things which are not seen are eternal" (2 Corinthians 4:17–18).

↤ First Impressions ↦

1. When have you faced hardship or deprivation? How did you respond?

2. Why did the Israelites rebel against Moses the second time, even after seeing God provide water once before? When have you done something similar?

3.	If you had been in Moses' place, how would you have reacted to the Israelites in the second waterless episode?

4.	Why did the Lord allow the people to get thirsty in the first place? What were His purposes in bringing water from the rock?

~ Some Key Principles ~

Jesus is the Rock of our salvation.

The Lord provided water for His thirsting people by having Moses strike a rock with his staff. This provided a picture of Christ, who was smitten by the rod of God's holy wrath—the Perfect Man smitten for the sins of others. His blood flowed forth, providing the water of salvation to those who were dying of spiritual thirst.

As Jesus told the Samaritan woman in John 4:13, "Whoever drinks of this water [from the well] will thirst again, but whoever drinks of the water that I shall give him will never thirst. But the water that I shall give him will become in him a fountain of water springing up into everlasting life."

Those who embrace Jesus Christ as their Lord and Savior, wholly trusting in His sacrificial work on the cross, can be certain that they have been forgiven from sin and given eternal life. "And this is eternal life, that they may know You, the only true God, and Jesus Christ whom You have sent" (John 17:3).

God's people must not take His commands lightly.

Moses' life was characterized by faith and power—although he was once described as more "humble . . . than all men who were on the face of the earth" (Numbers 12:3)—and he is listed in Hebrews as one of the great people of God. But even he was not exempt from God's discipline, and the Lord expected him to be an example to the people of what it means to obey the word of the Lord. When he disobeyed the Lord's command to speak to the rock, he disqualified himself from entering the promised land—a result that caused him deep grief.

From the human perspective, it seemed like a very small failure when Moses struck the rock the second time. After all, he was under great duress from the Israelites' rebellion and complaints, and it is not surprising that he lost his temper once or twice. But the Lord expected Moses to be an example of obedience for the Israelites. God always holds those in leadership positions to a higher degree of accountability, expecting His undershepherds to be examples of faithfulness and obedience for others.

We do not know the larger implications of the Lord's work in our lives and circumstances. He may well be using your present situation to bring glory to Himself in ways that you never dreamed of. But whatever our situation, we must not take His commands lightly.

Our grumbling can have a negative effect on others.

The people of Israel were constantly complaining during their exodus from Egypt. Even though the Lord had demonstrated His power and grace again and again, miraculously preserving them from their enemies and providing for their every need—they continuously accused Him of treachery.

It is a natural human response to complain when things go wrong in life. But whenever we do so, we are actually saying that we do not trust the Lord's sovereignty in our lives. We express a fear that He will prove unfaithful, that He is not worthy of our trust and obedience. And even small words of complaint can influence the people around us to stop trusting the Lord in their own lives. For that reason, Paul instructed us to "do all things without complaining and disputing," that we may become "children of God without fault in the midst of a crooked and perverse generation, among whom [we] shine as lights in the world, holding fast the word of life" (Philippians 2:14–16).

⌁ Digging Deeper ⌁

5. *Why did God treat Moses' sin so severely? How did He show His grace?*

6. *In what way did Moses fail to treat God as holy in front of the people? Why do you think Moses was held to such a strict accountability for his actions?*

7. In what ways is Christ pictured in the rock that provided water? How does the apostle Paul use this illustration in 1 Corinthians 10:1–4?

8. God never abandoned the nation of Israel, despite the people's constant complaining. What does this teach us about God's character? About His faithfulness?

⤳ TAKING IT PERSONALLY ⤳

9. How much does grumbling characterize your response to hardship? How might your words and attitude be influencing others?

10. In what areas is the Lord calling you to trust Him more fully? In what areas is He calling you to greater obedience?

BEZALEL AND AHOLIAB

✍ CHARACTERS' BACKGROUND ✍

The Lord has gathered the Israelites near Mount Sinai, and He is giving Moses explicit instructions on how the people are to live and worship God. These instructions include detailed plans on building a portable tabernacle that the people will use for worship during their travels in the wilderness.

The tabernacle consisted of a portable wall of cloth that created a rectangular space. Inside that space were many articles of furniture, plus a tent that housed the Holy Place and the Most Holy Place. Inside the Most Holy Place was the ark of the covenant, a gorgeous and ornate box with golden angels carved on top. These many elements of the tabernacle would require a great wealth of raw materials—gold, silver, bronze, rich textiles, precious gems—as well as skilled craftsmen to transform them according to God's blueprint.

Though the Israelites had lived for many generations as mere slaves making bricks, it is possible that some of them were employed as craftsmen and artisans in Egypt—as a necessary part of the construction crews used by Pharaoh. But whatever their level of training, God would now specially enable these craftsmen to build the tabernacle to His specific standards, such that the end product was of exceeding quality and beauty. The fact that they were able to construct something so exquisite while living in the wilderness bears testimony to the supernatural enablement they received from God.

The lesson that we will learn in these passages is that the Lord never commands us to do something without giving us the things we need. He provided the Israelites with a great wealth of materials when they left Egypt, and He endowed certain people with the skills that were needed for the construction. One of the greatest gifts of all is given freely to all Christians: the presence of God's Holy Spirit in our lives who enables us to do *whatever* God calls us to.

⤳ Reading Exodus 31:1–11 ⤳

Called by God: *The Lord has commanded the Israelites to build an elaborate tabernacle, and He calls out two men to oversee the construction.*

1. Then the Lord spoke to Moses: The Israelites were still encamped near Sinai, and Moses was meeting with the Lord on the mountain.

2. I have called by name: The Lord frequently demonstrated in the Old Testament that He knew His people by name, that He was acquainted with each person intimately. Later, Jesus added that the very hairs of our head are numbered (Matthew 10:30). We tend to focus on the "great" men and women of Scripture, figures such as Moses and Abraham and others, but there were a great many other men and women who faithfully served the Lord whose names may not appear in Scripture. Their service to God was as important and precious in His eyes as that of the "big names" of the Bible.

Bezalel: The name means "in the shadow of God." Jewish tradition has it that Bezalel was a young man at the time of his calling, but all we know for certain is what is recorded in these passages.

3. I have filled him with the Spirit of God: It was God's Spirit who provided Bezalel with the skill and wisdom needed to construct the tabernacle, and it was uncommon in the Old Testament period for people to be anointed by the Holy Spirit. Christians, however, are indwelt by God's Holy Spirit, and He endows His people with a wide variety of gifts designed for use in building the body of Christ.

in wisdom, in understanding, in knowledge, and in all manner of workmanship: This list of spiritual gifts from the Spirit is revealing. It is not surprising that the Holy Spirit would give us wisdom, understanding, and knowledge, but it is sometimes overlooked that He provides more practical "hands-on" skills as well. The Holy Spirit gave Bezalel the ability to perform "all manner of workmanship" in creating the things needed for the tabernacle, making him a skilled craftsman. The Lord provides His people with the gifts that are needed for His work.

Gifts from the Spirit: *Bezalel and Aholiab receive a special anointment of gifts from the Holy Spirit, equipping them to create all sorts of beautiful objects.*

4. artistic works: God's plan for the tabernacle included many intricate details, designed and created to the Lord's exact specifications. These included things created of precious metals and ornamented with precious stones, items crafted and carved from wood, and many articles of cloth. The people of Israel were called by God to create this beautiful tabernacle and its attendant furniture, and the design required craftsmen of the highest degree of skill. God provided His people with gifted people whom He had endowed with the artistic skills required.

6. AHOLIAB: The name means "tent of the Father." Again, all that we know of Aholiab is told in these passages.

I HAVE PUT WISDOM IN THE HEARTS: Wisdom means "exercising . . . sound judgment or discernment, especially in relation to conduct and the choice of means and ends; . . . characterized by good sense and prudence."[1] Imparting such wisdom is the chief role of the Holy Spirit in the lives of Christians as He teaches us to live like Christ and to conform to His image. The exercise of our spiritual gifts should always be characterized by wisdom and prudence.

11. ACCORDING TO ALL THAT I HAVE COMMANDED YOU THEY SHALL DO: The Lord never commands His people to do anything without also providing the means for obedience. In this case, He had commanded His people to construct a tabernacle of exceeding quality and beauty—so He also bestowed unique spiritual gifts upon certain individuals, which enabled them to construct each item.

⤳ READING EXODUS 35:30–36:7 ⤶

A TEAM EFFORT: *The work of creating the tabernacle is not to be undertaken by two men; it will require many others as well—in fact, it will involve the entire nation of Israel.*

31. HE HAS FILLED HIM WITH THE SPIRIT OF GOD: Only certain individuals in the Old Testament are described as "filled with the Spirit of God," as it was a unique anointing prior to Christ. But Jesus sent God's Holy Spirit to His people, and the Spirit now indwells all Christians. What's more, the Holy Spirit provides each believer with spiritual gifts that are to be used in the service of God.

34. THE ABILITY TO TEACH: The Lord also gave Bezalel and Aholiab skill in teaching their trades. This indicates that they were most probably the supervisors or leaders of the construction teams.

36:1. EVERY GIFTED ARTISAN: The Lord had evidently also sent His Spirit upon others in Israel at this time, equipping them also to do the skilled work required for the tabernacle. God, as He does even today, had perfectly gifted and equipped each individual for the task He had required of them: "For My yoke is easy and My burden is light" (Matthew 11:30).

[1] Lesley Brown, ed., *The New Shorter Oxford English Dictionary* (Oxford: Clarendon Press, 1993).

2. everyone whose heart was stirred: The Lord did not force His people into conscripted service; to do so would have merely turned Israel from one slavery to another. He called them to serve Him willingly, with a glad heart. He does the same today.

Freely Giving: *The people of Israel all join together to create God's tabernacle, using their gifts and possessions generously—even to the point of excess.*

3. the offering which the children of Israel had brought: All the people of Israel, not just Bezalel and Aholiab, participated in the construction of the tabernacle. There were other craftsmen who worked under the guidance of these two men, others who served the workmen in behind-the-scenes ministries, and the entire nation of Israel contributed the materials that were needed. Today, as then, God calls all His children to be actively involved in His great work. Furthermore, no job is more necessary than another for the final completion of the task. In the case of the tabernacle, if any particular function had not been done—crafting, supporting, providing materials—the work itself would not have been finished.

freewill offerings: Note that there was no compulsion for God's people to provide the materials for the tabernacle—the Lord relied entirely upon His people's generosity. Using one's gifts for God's service and sharing from one's material blessings should be a joy, not a grudging chore.

5. The people bring much more than enough: This was one of Israel's happier times, when the people poured out to God their gratitude for His countless blessings. This should be our response as well, giving generously and freely to God's work and to His people simply because we are grateful for all that He has given us.

6. the people were restrained from bringing: Literally, the people were "held back" from bringing any more gifts. The implication is that they had to be almost physically restrained, their zeal and generosity was so great.

ᗢ First Impressions ᗢ

1. *What roles did various people play in constructing the tabernacle? Who was included in the work?*

2.   If you had been present during this time, what role might you have played in the construction?

3.   Why did God give Bezalel and Aholiab the ability to teach others? What principle does this passage teach us about how God equips His people to accomplish His work?

4.   Why were the people so eager to give their material possessions for the tabernacle? What did this reveal about the character of God?

⌁ Some Key Principles ⌁

The Lord gives us what we need for His service.

The Lord had commanded the nation of Israel to create a portable tabernacle to use in worship during their travels in the wilderness, prior to entering Canaan. He gave Moses strict instructions on what to create, how to create it, and what it would look like when finished. Many of these articles, such as the ark of the covenant, were intricate and ornate, very beautiful works of art that required skill in metal smithing, gem cutting, textile weaving, and so forth.

The Israelites, however, had been simple slaves for many generations, and most of them had few skills beyond making bricks. Furthermore, they were living in the desert, carrying all their possessions in a huge caravan, and they did not have access to raw materials. But the Lord does not command us to do things that we cannot accomplish—although there are times when we cannot accomplish His work without the direct empowerment of His Holy Spirit. He gave a special endowment of gifts to specific individuals to perform the artistry, and He had already given the people of Israel great riches from the Egyptians that could be used for the raw materials.

This same principle applies to the Lord's people today. He gives us natural talents that can be used for His glory, and He provides spiritual gifts that are specifically designed to meet some need in the people around us. He even gives us the work that earns our income. And most of all, He gives us His Holy Spirit, who teaches us how to become more like Christ.

Those gifts—whether spiritual or material—are to be used for His glory, not our own. Bezalel and Aholiab were given special gifts from God, enabling them to be master craftsmen in a wide variety of trades—from working with metals to shaping precious stones to building ornate furniture and weaving gorgeous textiles. Such tremendous gifts could have made them both very wealthy men by creating beautiful objects for sale.

But that is not what these men used their gifts to do. They understood that the Lord had given them a special anointing for the specific purpose of creating His tabernacle, and the finished tabernacle would be for God's glory, not theirs. This does not mean that it is wrong to earn a living using the gifts and talents that the Lord has given—in fact, all good things come from His hand. But the Lord gives us gifts so that we can share them with others, not use them for our own gratification. "Even so you, since you are zealous for spiritual gifts, let it be for the edification of the church that you seek to excel" (1 Corinthians 14:12).

The Lord loves a cheerful giver.

It is very moving to picture the people of Israel, so eager to participate in building the Lord's tabernacle that they poured out their material goods like water. Every morning they came burdened with gold and silver and cloth and precious gems to be used as raw materials by the craftsmen.

It is true, of course, that they owned these possessions in the first place because God had given them favor in the eyes of the Egyptians, and they had been given the goods freely as the Israelites departed. Yet this fact may have been the very motivation behind the people's generosity: they recognized that they would not even own such precious possessions if the Lord had not provided them in the first place. The Israelites gave generously and freely, not under any compulsion, and they gave to the point that they had to be restrained from giving further.

This should be our attitude as well. We should always remember that our material possessions are all provided by the Lord—even the very income that we work for—and He wants us to share freely with others. "So let each one give as he purposes in his heart, not grudgingly or of necessity; for God loves a cheerful giver. And God is able to make all grace abound toward you, that you, always having all sufficiency in all things, may have an abundance for every good work" (2 Corinthians 9:7–8).

⌇ DIGGING DEEPER ⌇

5. What does it mean to be "filled with the Spirit of God"? What effect does such a filling have on a person's life? See Ephesians 5:18–21 for a New Testament passage identifying some of the results of a Spirit-filled life.

6. Why did God call Bezalel and Aholiab "by name"? What does this reveal about God's character? About our spiritual gifts?

7. What role does wisdom play in using our spiritual and material gifts? What might be an unwise use of those gifts?

8. How were all the roles of building the tabernacle equally necessary? Why do people sometimes think that some roles in spiritual service are more important than others?

ᨔ Taking It Personally ᨔ

9. What gifts—spiritual, innate, or material—has the Lord given you? How are you using them to bring glory to God?

10. Do you give to the Lord's work cheerfully or grudgingly? What motivates you to give?

~ 8 ~
BALAAM AND BALAK

~ HISTORICAL BACKGROUND ~

The Israelites had been wandering in the wilderness for many years, and they were finally camped near the Jordan River across from Jericho. They had recently destroyed several Canaanite armies, and the Lord's power was abundantly evident to the world around them. The nations of Canaan were afraid of God's people!

One of those nations was Moab, whose people were descended from Lot, and the Israelites were now camped in Moabite territory. Years ago, the Lord promised Lot that his descendants would enjoy an inheritance in the land of Canaan. He had, therefore, commanded the Israelites not to attack or disturb the Moabites, or even to touch any of the land belonging to Moab. The leaders of Moab, however, either didn't know about that injunction or placed no faith in it—they were afraid that Israel would destroy them, just as they had destroyed the surrounding nations.

One Moabite leader, named Balak, decided that if he couldn't defeat the Israelites with physical force, he would fight them on the spiritual plane. He hired a world-renowned pagan prophet named Balaam to cast a curse upon Israel. Balaam presents a picture of all those who dabble in the occult, and we discover that he was motivated not by a desire for truth but by a lust for monetary gain and worldly prestige. The occult is very real, but its powers are of the devil and will bring certain destruction upon those who practice them.

Fortunately, the power of God is far beyond the powers of the devil. What God blesses, no power on earth or in hell can curse.

~ READING NUMBERS 22:1–41 ~

MEANWHILE, IN MOAB . . . : *The story of Israel's wanderings in the wilderness shifts focus to show us what is happening in nearby Moab.*

1. Then the children of Israel moved: This story took place well into the forty years of Israel's wandering in the wilderness, after both Aaron and Miriam (Moses' sister) had died.

the plains of Moab: Near the Salt Sea (Dead Sea). See the map in the Introduction.

2. saw all that Israel had done to the Amorites: The Israelites had utterly defeated the neighbors of Moab. (See Numbers 21.)

3. Moab was sick with dread: The following passages are laden with irony—some that is humorous, much that is not. The sad irony of this verse was that the Israelites were forbidden by the Lord to attack the Moabites (Deuteronomy 2:9). They were the descendants of Lot, who were promised an inheritance in Canaan. Thus Balak had nothing to fear.

Introducing Balaam: *Balaam was a pagan false prophet who earned a nice profit by interceding with false gods. He was in for some surprises this time.*

5. Balaam the son of Beor: Balaam was a false prophet who practiced divination and sorcery. He was from Pethor, a city on the Euphrates River, perhaps near Mari, where the existence of a cult of prophets has been found whose activities resembled those of Balaam. Balaam practiced magic and divination and eventually led Israel into apostasy. Later Scripture identifies Balaam as a false prophet. (See 2 Peter 2:15–16 and Jude 11.)

6. curse this people for me: It is noteworthy that Balak immediately resorted to spiritism in hopes of defeating Israel. He had already recognized that the victories of Israel were due to the power of God, not to the strength of their army. Even so, Balak tried to fight the hand of God rather than submit to it.

he whom you curse is cursed: A curse was an *imprecation*, words that allegedly called down the anger of the gods upon another person. Balaam apparently had a reputation for uttering curses that really worked.

9. God came to Balaam: Balaam did not worship the Lord; he served the pagan gods of Canaan. Moreover, he made a tidy living charging fees for his services (Numbers 22:7), and those services amounted to manipulating the supposed powers of his false gods to serve his own needs. It is astonishing, therefore, that the Lord chose to appear to him at all. Balaam had no authority whatsoever to summon God this way; it is yet another demonstration of God's grace that He was even willing to speak to Balaam.

12. You shall not go with them: The Lord mercifully gave Balaam clear instructions on what to do, when He might just as easily have slain him on the spot. Balaam should have recognized at this moment that he was speaking to the true God rather than to the shams and false idols he had served in the past. He then could have humbled himself before the Lord and found grace; instead, he continued to serve the god that he had always served: money.

YOU SHALL NOT CURSE THE PEOPLE, FOR THEY ARE BLESSED: The Lord had promised Abraham, "I will bless those who bless you, and I will curse him who curses you; and in you all the families of the earth shall be blessed" (Genesis 12:3).

UPPING THE ANTE: *Balak evidently knows Balaam's character and what motivates him. If Balaam won't come with the first offer, Balak will simply raise the price.*

13. THE LORD HAS REFUSED TO GIVE ME PERMISSION: If the story had ended here, Balaam (and Israel) would have been better off. But the devil has many wiles, and Balaam's temptation was not over.

15. MORE NUMEROUS AND MORE HONORABLE: Balak was determined to seduce Balaam to carry out his plan, so he resorted to flattery by sending emissaries who were more impressive—higher heads of state and glamorous celebrities, as it were. He evidently knew his man and understood what would get Balaam's attention. In fact, he may have assumed that Balaam's first refusal was merely a ploy to get more attention and a better fee. These things suggest that Balaam's selfish motives were well known.

18. THOUGH BALAK WERE TO GIVE ME HIS HOUSE FULL OF SILVER AND GOLD, I COULD NOT GO BEYOND THE WORD OF THE LORD MY GOD: This is very far from the truth. First off, the Lord was *not* the God whom Balaam served. And second, Balaam would soon sell his services for much less than a "house full of silver and gold." Finally, his wheedling and bargaining with God demonstrate that he was not afraid to go against the Lord's directions.

THE LORD MY GOD: At first glance, it would seem that Balaam had humbled himself before the Lord and now served Him as God. But actions speak louder than words, and, again, his subsequent decisions demonstrate that his words were a mere sham. It is probable that Balaam was merely trying to impress his visitors by claiming to speak for yet another god.

19. WHAT MORE THE LORD WILL SAY: The Lord had already been emphatic in His instructions, so there was no need to ask a second time. But Balaam was sorely tempted by Balak's offer, and he was trying to wheedle God into letting him go.

20. RISE AND GO WITH THEM: Once again we see the grace of the Lord in His relations with humans—even with a man who did not truly acknowledge Him as God. The Lord relented to the point of allowing Balaam to go and earn his fee—but He warned him that he must take care to speak only what he was told.

BALAAM'S DONKEY: *Balaam has hardened his heart against God, just as Pharaoh had done, and is motivated only by greed. His donkey will prove to be wiser than he.*

22. GOD'S ANGER WAS AROUSED BECAUSE HE WENT: Balaam thought he could fool God in the same way that he fooled men, by pretending to have one motivation while pursuing another. The Lord knew, however, that he fully intended to curse Israel in order to earn the highest fee, so He appeared to him unexpectedly in order to drive home His command. This time, Balaam got the message.

AS AN ADVERSARY AGAINST HIM: God had previously appeared to Balaam in a somewhat compliant role, coming before him when summoned. Balaam did not realize, however, that this was due to the mercy of God, not to some power that he wielded. In this confrontation, Balaam learned more about the character of the one true God.

23. THE DONKEY SAW THE ANGEL OF THE LORD: There is a delicious irony in the fact that Balaam, the world-renowned manipulator of the gods, could not even see what was evident to a donkey.

28. THE LORD OPENED THE MOUTH OF THE DONKEY: Even in His role as Balaam's adversary, the Lord still demonstrated His grace—even going to the point of working a wonderful miracle on Balaam's behalf.

29. YOU HAVE ABUSED ME: Literally, "you have made a fool of me." This was far truer than Balaam realized, for a donkey was about to instruct him in wisdom.

A SWORD IN MY HAND: Here is another humorous irony. Balaam did not realize that there was indeed a sword nearby, but it was in the hand of an angel—and its potential victim was *not* the donkey!

31. FELL FLAT ON HIS FACE: Balaam was a diviner, a person who dabbles in the magical arts, playing with forbidden powers that he did not understand. For the first time in his life, he found himself face-to-face with the power of the one true God, and he was literally floored.

YOUR WAY IS PERVERSE: *The Lord opens Balaam's eyes so that he can finally see the truth. His desire for monetary gain is perverse in the Lord's eyes.*

32. YOUR WAY IS PERVERSE BEFORE ME: The word translated "perverse" literally means "to push headlong or to drive recklessly." Balaam had heard the Lord's command not to curse Israel—indeed, not even to go with Balak's men—but he was stubbornly pushing forward just the same. He was literally running ahead of the Lord, seeking his own way rather than waiting for the Lord's guidance—or obeying it when he got it.

33. SURELY I WOULD ALSO HAVE KILLED YOU BY NOW: The Lord explicitly told Balaam that the only reason the false prophet was still breathing was because He had been extending His mercy. By all rights, the Lord might just as easily have killed Balaam long before this.

34. IF IT DISPLEASES YOU: Even when face-to-face with the Angel of the Lord, Balaam persisted in being disingenuous. He already knew that it displeased God, yet he was stubbornly insisting upon having his own way.

35. GO WITH THE MEN: Balaam, like Pharaoh, had already hardened his heart toward God. His god was money, and he was only willing to obey his drive toward profit. The Lord had told him what to do, but he had obstinately insisted upon going with Balak's men, so the Lord permitted him to continue on his way—but with the reiterated warning not to curse Israel. In the end, as we shall see, he found a way to disobey this command as well.

41. BROUGHT HIM UP TO THE HIGH PLACES OF BAAL: It is significant that Balaam looked upon Israel from the high places of Baal, worship sites that were dedicated to Canaan's false god. Balaam's entire outlook on life was from the perspective of Baal, rather than the perspective of God, and he remained spiritually blind for the rest of his life. Even his donkey was wiser than he.

⌁ READING NUMBERS 23:8–30; 25:1–3 ⌁

THE ORACLES OF BALAAM: *Balaam stands in the high place of Baal and pronounces not curses, but blessings on Israel. The Lord uses the mouth of a pagan to speak truth.*

23:8. HOW SHALL I CURSE WHOM GOD HAS NOT CURSED: This is a tremendous truth for God's people: those whom God has blessed cannot be cursed. The world, other people, even the devil himself cannot bring lasting harm to those under the blessing of God.

9. FROM THE TOP OF THE ROCKS I SEE HIM: It is wonderful also to realize that Balaam was standing in the highest place of Canaan's primary false god—and even from that elevated position of wicked power, he could do nothing to harm God's people.

NOT RECKONING ITSELF AMONG THE NATIONS: God's people are separate from the world around them; they are not part of the world's system.

10. WHO CAN COUNT THE DUST OF JACOB?: The Lord had promised Abraham, "I will make your descendants as the dust of the earth; so that if a man could number the dust of the earth, then your descendants also could be numbered" (Genesis 13:16).

Let me die the death of the righteous: This may have been a sincere wish of Balaam, but it did not come to pass. He may have desired the reward of the righteous, but he lived the life of the self-serving. His end was the death of the wicked.

19. God is not a man, that He should lie: Balaam's second oracle is a wonderful revelation of God's character. He never lies, and His promises never fail. "Oh, the depth of the riches both of the wisdom and knowledge of God! How unsearchable are His judgments and His ways past finding out! *'For who has known the mind of the Lord? Or who has become His counselor?' 'Or who has first given to Him and it shall be repaid to Him?'* For of Him and through Him and to Him are all things, to whom be glory forever" (Romans 11:33–36).

20. He has blessed, and I cannot reverse it: The most intimidating power on earth—even the power of the devil—cannot reverse God's blessing. Once He has blessed His people, they can never again be cursed.

23. there is no sorcery against Jacob: Balaam and Balak believed that they could use sorcery and other forbidden magical practices to bring a curse against God's people, but they were only using the devil's tools—and those tools are utterly powerless against God's people.

Oh, what God has done: The majesty of God's sovereign work leaves one speechless. God's ways are glorious and beyond the comprehension of man.

Balaam Earns His Filthy Profit: *Balaam was not permitted to openly curse Israel, but he found another way of earning his money: he advised Moab to seduce Israel to sin.*

25:1. Israel remained in Acacia Grove: The focus now shifts from Balaam, standing atop the high places of Baal, to the people of Israel in the plain below. What follows took place not long after Balaam uttered his oracles.

the people began to commit harlotry with the women of Moab: The people of Moab undertook this plan deliberately, based on advice that Balaam gave to Balak (Numbers 31:16). In the end, Balaam was not able to openly speak a curse against Israel, but he earned his filthy profit by counseling the Moabites to undermine Israel's sexual morals. The devil still works this way today, seducing God's people into embracing the ways of the world.

2. They invited the people to the sacrifices: These sacrifices included fertility rites involving sexual immorality. Though God's people are not to be unfriendly to non-Christians, neither are we to adopt their ways and perspectives. "Do you not know that friendship with the world is enmity with God? Whoever therefore wants to be a friend of the world makes himself an enemy of God" (James 4:4).

↶ First Impressions ↷

1. Why did Balak hire Balaam to curse Israel? In what ways was this a very foolish deed?

2. What motivated Balaam?

3. Why was Balaam unable to curse Israel?

4. How did Balaam finally earn his money?

⌁ Some Key Principles ⌁

No power on earth or in hell can stand against God's blessing.

Balaam wanted very much to cast a curse upon God's people—it was how he earned his living, and he stood to make a handsome profit from the people of Moab. He even represented supposedly powerful false gods like Baal and had every advantage the world could bring to bear against Israel. Yet he was unable to pronounce anything other than a blessing.

God has placed His blessing upon those who are redeemed by the blood of Christ. When He looks upon us, He views us through that filter—He sees only the holiness of Jesus, not our sins and shortcomings. There is nothing on earth or in hell or even in heaven itself which can ever undo God's blessing upon His people. What Christ accomplished on the cross can never be undone.

"I am persuaded that neither death nor life, nor angels nor principalities nor powers, nor things present nor things to come, nor height nor depth, nor any other created thing, shall be able to separate us from the love of God which is in Christ Jesus our Lord" (Romans 8:38–39).

God's people must stand guard against the temptations of the world.

The opposite side to the first key principle is that even Christians are in constant danger of falling into the world's sinful pattern. The devil lays many traps to ensnare God's people. He cannot have our souls, but he can lead us into error if we do not stand guard.

Balaam recognized this truth, and he taught the Moabites how to seduce God's people through their pagan practices. The Israelites fell into the temptation of sexual immorality thanks to Balaam's advice. Balaam himself was led to destruction through his own love of money and perhaps his fear of men. But Jesus said, "My friends, do not be afraid of those who kill the body, and after that have no more that they can do. But I will show you whom you should fear: Fear Him who, after He has killed, has power to cast into hell; yes, I say to you, fear Him!" (Luke 12:4–5).

Peter also had a dire warning for those who would follow God: "Be sober, be vigilant; because your adversary the devil walks about like a roaring lion, seeking whom he may devour. Resist him, steadfast in the faith, knowing that the same sufferings are experienced by your brotherhood in the world" (1 Peter 5:8–9).

Do not dabble in the occult.

Balaam was just one of many false prophets in Canaan during his day. These people used various forms of magic and sorcery to speak with false gods (demons) and to "tap into" the power of the spirit realm. What they didn't know, however, was that they were not interacting with any gods at all, but rather with the power of Satan.

Interest in the occult is on the rise in Western society today, and even Christians are being lured into dabbling with "spirit guides," "channeling," horoscopes, praying to angels, and other elements of magic. These things are not innocent toys to play with, nor are they legitimate powers that mankind has at his disposal. They are forms of sorcery, and the power behind them is the devil.

God forbids His people from any contact with such things. "There shall not be found among you anyone who . . . practices witchcraft, or a soothsayer, or one who interprets omens, or a sorcerer, or one who conjures spells, or a medium, or a spiritist, or one who calls up the dead. For all who do these things are an abomination to the LORD" (Deuteronomy 18:10–12).

⌒ DIGGING DEEPER ⌒

5.   What does God reveal of His character in these passages? What do we learn of human nature?

6.   Why did God use a pagan false prophet to speak truth? What does this reveal about His sovereignty?

7. How might the Israelites have avoided sin with the Moabites? What could they have done to stand firm against that temptation?

8. What temptations does the world offer that can lead Christians away from God? What can Christians do to protect themselves? See Ephesians 6:10–18 for a helpful starting point.

⤳ TAKING IT PERSONALLY ⤳

9. List areas of the occult that are popular in the world today. How should Christians respond to such things?

10. Review the list of things that cannot separate us from God's love (Romans 8:38–39). Which of these is most meaningful to you? Spend time praising God for His great love.

～ 9 ～
JOSHUA AND CALEB

～ CHARACTERS' BACKGROUND ～

The Israelites had recently left Egypt and had now arrived at the Jordan River, the border to the promised land. God had faithfully and dramatically kept His promise to deliver them from bondage, and now He was about to fulfill His promise to give them a land flowing with milk and honey. Moses sent twelve men, one from each tribe of Israel, to spy out the land and plan a military strategy.

The problem was that the land was already populated. What's more, the people who lived there were very powerful—and some of them were giants! It's true that the land was very fertile— it took two men to carry a bunch of grapes—but how were the people of Israel to defeat those powerful armies? This, at least, was the perspective of ten of the spies—but two of the spies saw things differently. Those two were Joshua and Caleb.

Joshua had been serving as Moses' personal assistant during the trek from Egypt; we know very little about Caleb's background. But background is not what matters at this time; what's important is one's attitude toward God. Yes, these were powerful armies and walled cities—and even some giants—but God was more powerful than they; He could and would conquer them, just as He had already conquered Pharaoh's army. His word was true concerning the richness of the land; His word would also prove true concerning the enemies who lived there.

This is what Joshua and Caleb focused on, and they demonstrated that they had complete faith in the character of God. They proved to be men of great courage, and we can learn much from their attitude.

～ READING NUMBERS 13:16–14:38 ～

SPYING OUT THE LAND: *The Israelites have arrived at the Jordan River not long after leaving Egypt, and Moses sends twelve men to spy out the promised land.*

13:16. THE MEN WHOM MOSES SENT TO SPY OUT THE LAND: The Israelites had been traveling through the wilderness, safe now from any pursuing armies, and had arrived at the Jordan River. As they looked across the river at the promised land, they were certain that their exodus from Egypt was nearly over. But before they could enter the land of milk and honey, they wanted to see what the enemy within was made of. So Moses sent twelve men—one from each tribe of Israel—across the Jordan to spy out the land and prepare a strategy for beginning their conquest of Canaan.

HOSHEA THE SON OF NUN: Moses changed the name of Hoshea, which means "desire for salvation," to Joshua, which means "the Lord is salvation." The difference in meaning is subtle but significant. The young man had originally desired salvation, and now he had found it in the Lord Himself. The fact that Moses changed his name indicates that Joshua was already under his close supervision. The name Jesus is another form of Joshua.

17. SPY OUT THE LAND OF CANAAN: Moses never doubted that the Lord would provide victory for His people as they entered Canaan, and his intention in sending out these spies was to plan strategy—not to determine whether or not they could defeat their enemies. The Lord wants His people to trust Him in all things, but we are also called to live responsibly—including planning ahead as much as is humanly possible.

20. BE OF GOOD COURAGE: This is actually a command, not a mere formulaic statement such as "have a nice day." Moses was commanding the spies to be courageous men, warning them in advance not to become overwhelmed with the obstacles that stood between them and their possession of Canaan. Courage is more than an emotion; it is a deliberate choice, choosing not to allow fear to take command. Most of the spies, however, would fail in this matter.

20. THE SEASON OF THE FIRST RIPE GRAPES: That is, mid-July.

21. WILDERNESS OF ZIN: See the map in the introduction. Rehob was northwest of the Sea of Galilee, not shown on the map. The spies covered the entire area of the promised land.

WHAT THEY FOUND THERE: *The spies spend forty days traveling throughout the land of Canaan and return with reports and grapes. BIG grapes!*

---

22. HEBRON: See the map in the introduction. This city was of importance to the Israelites because Abraham had built an altar there and because both he and Isaac were buried there. The city had since been fortified by Canaanites.

THE DESCENDANTS OF ANAK: The descendants of Anak were renowned for their great stature, much as Goliath would one day become famous for his size among the

Philistines. Ahiman, Sheshai, and Talmai were probably specific men living in Hebron at the time. They may have been famous warriors themselves.

23. THEY CARRIED IT BETWEEN TWO OF THEM ON A POLE: This demonstrates the enormous size and weight of the grapes, as it required two men to carry one simple bunch. Here was tangible proof of the Lord's promise that the promised land would be abundantly wealthy and comfortable for the people.

26. SHOWED THEM THE FRUIT OF THE LAND: The spies were accountable before the Lord for the report they brought back, because their encouragement or discouragement would influence the nation as a whole. Nevertheless, all the people could see for themselves that the Lord's words were true: the land was indeed flowing with milk and honey.

27. IT TRULY FLOWS WITH MILK AND HONEY: Thus far, the report of the spies was true—at least factually accurate. But what mattered more was their faith in the future, their confidence that God would conquer the land on their behalf. Had they rejoiced in the fruit rather than lamenting over the giants, their report might have been different.

AND NOW FOR THE BAD NEWS: *The spies have presented all the good report and have been factually accurate. Now they focus on the problems—and end up departing from fact.*

28. NEVERTHELESS: Here is the actual *spirit* of the spies' report. Their facts were accurate—the land did flow with milk and honey—but their focus was all wrong. They chose to become obsessed with the obstacles that were in their way rather than trusting in the power and promises of God.

29. AMALEKITES ... HITTITES ... JEBUSITES: None of this was unexpected news to the people. The Lord had already told Moses that there were people living in the land of Canaan (Exodus 3:8). Furthermore, He had promised that He would drive out these nations before the Israelites, giving them victory after victory over their enemies. But the people chose to act as though the Lord had not warned them of these people, as if God Himself were caught by surprise or had deliberately sent them to be slaughtered.

30. CALEB QUIETED THE PEOPLE: Caleb demonstrated his leadership abilities here by taking charge when the entire nation of Israel was beginning to rise against Moses.

WE ARE WELL ABLE TO OVERCOME IT: He also demonstrated that he had complete faith in God's promises. He did not pretend that there were no problems to overcome, but he chose to focus on ways to overcome the obstacles (by focusing on God), rather than on the obstacles themselves.

31. THEY ARE STRONGER THAN WE: This was probably true, in military terms. But Pharaoh's elite army was far stronger than the Israelites—indeed, they were stronger than the strongest army that yet remained in the promised land—and the Lord had utterly destroyed them. The ten spies were placing their faith in their own power, not in the power of God.

32. A BAD REPORT: In this, the ten spies sinned greatly. Their report focused on the enemies that needed to be defeated rather than on the power of God to defeat those enemies. It also stirred up fear in the people, expressing that the spies themselves did not believe that God could be trusted. Their report led the entire nation to lose faith in God and to despair.

A LAND THAT DEVOURS ITS INHABITANTS: This is simply not true. At this point, the spies were bringing a blatantly false report that contradicted the concrete evidence they had brought back—grapes that were so heavy that two men were needed to carry them.

ALL THE PEOPLE WHOM WE SAW: This, too, was false. There were indeed some giants in the land, but they were probably the exception rather than the rule. When we focus on the problems that confront us rather than on God's power and faithfulness, we begin to exaggerate the problems and are soon overcome with doubt and anxiety.

33. AND SO WE WERE IN THEIR SIGHT: This is another side effect of losing our focus: we begin to worry too much about what other people think and too little about what God thinks. The Canaanites might have considered the Israelites of no consequence, but God thought otherwise. They may also have thought that they could defeat and subjugate Israel, but God knew that they could not overcome His power. The actual fact is that the people of Canaan probably did *not* think these things in the first place, for the fear of God had swept over the nations in that area as God led the Israelites from victory to victory.

THE ISRAELITES DESPAIR: *The bad report of the spies leads the entire nation of Israel to lose sight of God's faithfulness. Despair and fear set in.*

14:1. ALL THE CONGREGATION: Here we see the effect of the negative report that the ten spies brought back. As those who had been put in a position of influence, their fear and doubt soon infected the entire nation. Their response was indicative of their rebellious hearts, which lacked faith in God's clear promises.

2. IF ONLY WE HAD DIED IN THIS WILDERNESS: Tragically, that is precisely what happened to those people because of this very incident.

3. WHY HAS THE LORD BROUGHT US TO THIS LAND TO FALL BY THE SWORD?: The people had made this false accusation against God many times before, as we have seen in previous studies. The Lord had wrought countless miracles, defeated powerful foes, removed immovable obstacles, provided for all their physical needs, traveled with them as a shady cloud and light-giving fire, met with them repeatedly to teach them about Himself, and even provided a worship place that moved with them wherever they went—all this and much more—yet the people accused Him of being treacherous. But we must remember that we are no different from the Israelites. God's people commit this same sin today when we forget all His blessings and accuse Him of not caring about our circumstances.

JOSHUA AND CALEB: *Two of the spies, however, refuse to succumb to the despair of the other ten. These two are Joshua and Caleb.*

6. TORE THEIR CLOTHES: Of the twelve spies, only Joshua and Caleb urged the people to trust God and move forward. They tore their clothes as an outward sign of their deep grief and frustration.

7. AN EXCEEDINGLY GOOD LAND: Joshua and Caleb focused on the blessings of God's promised land rather than on the obstacles. It is interesting that all twelve men had the same basic facts to work from, but Joshua and Caleb reached a radically different conclusion. The reason is not in the facts but in the faith. There are times when obedience to God will seem very hard, maybe even impossible; in those instances, we must rely on His character and His promises, choosing to trust and obey him even when it is difficult to do so.

8. HE WILL BRING US INTO THIS LAND AND GIVE IT TO US: Here is the nub of Joshua and Caleb's thinking, and it is the opposite of the other spies' opinion. The ten focused on their own strength, while Joshua and Caleb focused on God's strength.

9. DO NOT REBEL AGAINST THE LORD, NOR FEAR THE PEOPLE OF THE LAND: When we focus on our circumstances, we begin to fear what other people can do to us. This is the same as rebelling against God, according to Joshua and Caleb. Fear is the result of taking our eyes away from God's faithfulness, and it leads us to rebel against Him.

THEY ARE OUR BREAD: The ten spies had said that they were like grasshoppers in the sight of the Canaanites. Joshua and Caleb retorted by stating emphatically that God's people would devour the giants like pieces of bread.

DO NOT FEAR THEM: Once again we see a commandment concerning fear. We tend to think of fear as an emotion, and as such, beyond our conscious control. But God's Word states repeatedly that we must *choose* not to permit fear to rule our thoughts. When fear rises in our hearts, we must conquer it with our wills by deliberately choosing to place our faith in Him.

GOD'S JUDGMENT FALLS: *The Lord responds to the people's rebellion, decreeing that an entire generation shall not see the promised land—except for Joshua and Caleb.*

22. WHO HAVE SEEN MY GLORY AND THE SIGNS WHICH I DID: The Lord laid out the sins of the people: they had seen His miracles and faithfulness repeatedly, yet they had just as repeatedly put Him to the test and refused to heed His voice. Allowing the Israelites to see the strength of their foes should have tested—and proven—the faith of the people to trust God in all things; instead, they put *Him* to the test. They did not heed His voice by obeying His repeated injunction to "move forward;" instead, they balked at His command and chose to move backward to Egypt. It is a grievous sin to rebel against the Lord.

23. THEY CERTAINLY SHALL NOT SEE THE LAND: As a result of this rebellion, the adults (age twenty and older) throughout the land of Israel were not permitted to enter the promised land. Instead, they wandered about the wilderness for the next forty years until every one of them had died—everyone except Joshua and Caleb.

24. HE HAS A DIFFERENT SPIRIT IN HIM: Caleb and Joshua demonstrated that they were obedient to the Spirit of God. The rest of the people were constantly submitting themselves to a spirit of fear.

38. JOSHUA ... AND CALEB ... REMAINED ALIVE: The Lord rewarded these two men for their faithfulness by exempting them from the tragic judgment that fell upon the rest of the nation. They set an example of what it means to trust God in all circumstances, focusing on His faithfulness rather than on circumstances.

↪ FIRST IMPRESSIONS ↩

1. *If you had been one of the spies, how would you have reacted to seeing giants? To strong, walled cities? To huge grapes?*

2. *Why did the ten spies say they could not defeat their enemies? Why did they not rejoice in the wealth of the land?*

3. Why did Joshua and Caleb say that the Israelites could defeat their enemies? How was their focus different from the others'?

4. If you had been in the Israelite camp, which report do you think you would have listened to?

↶ Some Key Principles ↶

Our mental focus affects our faith.

Twelve men walked throughout the land of Canaan. They all saw the same things: giants, walled cities, immense grapes, and so forth. Ten of those men, however, determined that Israel could never conquer the land, whereas two were convinced that it would be an easy matter to move in and take possession.

The difference lay in what the spies focused on. Ten of them admitted that there were lots of big grapes, but their main concern was with the giants and walled cities. They were focused on the problems that lay ahead of them—and their *own* strength to overcome those problems. Joshua and Caleb, on the other hand, were focused not on the immediate obstacles but on the prize that lay beyond those obstacles. They were concentrating solely on God's power and faithfulness in the past, and that is what convinced them that they could devour their enemies like bread.

This kind of faith is not the power of "positive thinking"; it is a conscious decision—often repeated—to place our trust in God's provision rather than in the problems that stand in our way. God's people are frequently faced with seemingly insurmountable obstacles, but the Lord calls us to rely on His strength, not our own, to overcome them. "He Himself has said, '*I will never leave you nor forsake you.*' So we may boldly say: '*The Lord is my helper; I will not fear. What can man do to me?*'" (Hebrews 13:5b–6).

We must *choose* to "be of good courage."

God's Word frequently commands us to "be of good courage" and "fear not." And these *are* commands, not suggestions or mere words of encouragement. True, the emotion of fear can come upon us at times, whether we will it or not, but what we do with that fear *is* a matter of will—and of obedience to God's command.

Joshua and Caleb saw the same giants that the other ten spies saw. They examined the same walled cities, observed the same trained enemy armies—yet they came to a radically different conclusion. The reason was that these two men deliberately resisted and overcame their fear, while the other ten fell prey to it.

This principle goes hand in hand with the previous one: our mental focus affects our faith. By consciously focusing our minds on the promises and character of God, not on the "odds," our faith is strengthened and enlarged. We are better able to resist fear, because we remember the many ways that God has been faithful in the past. It becomes easier and easier to choose to trust Him because if He was faithful in the past, He will be faithful in the future. It's consistent with His character. That's the mindset we must have, and it is a *choice*. To resist fear is also a choice. We resist it simply by *choosing* to trust God instead.

Our lack of faith may lead others into sin.

It is quite likely that all the way back to camp, the ten negative spies infected one another with their fear and lack of faith, reiterating to each other all the terrible dangers that lay in Canaan. It should come as no surprise, then, that when they brought their words of discouragement to the people of Israel, the entire nation was infected by their doubt and negativity.

Focusing on circumstances rather than on God—thereby *losing our faith* in His promises—is a sin. That sin is compounded when our lack of faith infects others. The things that we say matter—our words affect our *own* attitudes, and they also affect the opinions of those around us. If our speech is filled with fear and woe, we will influence others to be filled with fear and woe. But if our speech is filled with an expectation of God's faithfulness, others will be encouraged to trust Him.

Just as we choose how to respond to fear, so also we must choose how to respond to trouble. The Lord permitted the Israelites to face hardships and enemies from time to time in order to test their faith—to strengthen it, just as steel is strengthened by testing. Our faith is strengthened each time we trust God, and we strengthen the faith of others by showing forth our own faith in Him.

⌁ DIGGING DEEPER ⌁

5. What role did the ten spies play in the despair of the nation? What role did each individual play?

6. Why are we commanded to "be of good courage"? How is this done? How can a person overcome fear, in practical terms?

7. List some of the things that God had done previously to prove to the people that He was in control. Why did these things not matter to the Israelites in this passage?

8. List some things that the Lord has done in your own life to prove that He is in control. How can these past victories help you as you face present or future difficulties?

ᦸ Taking It Personally ᦸ

9. When have you been affected by someone else's attitude toward hardship? When has your attitude affected others?

10. What do you tend to focus on when circumstances go awry? On a practical level, how can you deepen your trust in God's faithfulness?

SECTION 3:

THEMES

In This Section:

PASSOVER

∽ THEMATIC BACKGROUND ∽

We are now returning to the time just prior to Israel's leaving Egypt. The Lord had sent nine plagues upon Pharaoh, each one more drastic than the last—but Pharaoh had not relented; his heart was still hardened against God, and he would not permit the Israelites to leave. The Lord had consistently extended grace to the people of Egypt, but the day of grace does eventually end. It was about to end for Egypt, and God was preparing to pour out His wrath.

The Lord commanded Moses and the people of Israel to prepare themselves for this calamitous event. Just as He had spared Israel from the devastating plagues, so He would now spare them from the most devastating of all: the death of every firstborn in the land. But this safety was not guaranteed—the people of God were required to *do* something to protect themselves from the wrath of God. That protection would come in the form of blood, the blood of an innocent lamb, sprinkled on the doorposts of their houses.

The Passover feast has been observed by the Jewish people around the world for thousands of years, ever since their exodus from Egypt. In this study, we will learn where that feast originated and what its important symbols mean. Most importantly, we will discover the profundity of the sacrificial lamb as it prefigures the greatest Lamb of all.

∽ READING EXODUS 12:1–51 ∽

THE PASSOVER LAMB: *The Lord commands Moses and the Israelites to commemorate their redemption from Egypt by sacrificing a lamb.*

1. IN THE LAND OF EGYPT: We have returned to the time when the Israelites were slaves in Egypt. By now, the Lord had sent nine plagues upon Pharaoh, but he had only hardened his heart, every time. The final plague was about to descend.

2. THE FIRST MONTH OF THE YEAR: The Lord instructed the Israelites to reestablish their calendar, with the new year beginning in the present month (March/April in the Western calendar). The Lord would later establish an annual feast day to commemorate this event, a feast that Jews still observe today. The Lord intended that Passover should always be inextricably linked to Israel's redemption from Egypt. Jesus, at the Last Supper, commanded the disciples to begin keeping a similar observance, known today as Communion or the Lord's Table. This ordinance commemorates Christians' redemption from sin.

3. A LAMB: The Lord had not yet given Moses the Law, so the sacrificial system had not yet been established. But from the beginning, the Lord demanded the sacrifice of an innocent lamb without blemish.

A LAMB FOR A HOUSEHOLD: Each household was commanded to obey the Lord's instructions in this matter. (In the same way today, each person must embrace the sacrifice of Christ for himself.) Those who refused to obey the Lord's command faced dire consequences, as we shall see.

4. TOO SMALL FOR THE LAMB: The Passover was to be available freely to all; no household was excluded. In the same way, the blood of Christ, which offers redemption from sin, is freely available to all who believe the gospel—no person is ineligible, and no sin is too great to be covered.

5. WITHOUT BLEMISH: The people were not to select a second-rate lamb for the sacrifice; only the very best would be acceptable. It was, in fact, to be *spotless*. Jesus was the only One who could pay the price for sin, the only *acceptable* sacrifice, because He was spotless, that is, *without sin*. "You were not redeemed with corruptible things, like silver or gold, . . . but with the precious blood of Christ, as of a lamb without blemish and without spot" (1 Peter 1:18–19). "[Christ] was in all points tempted as we are, *yet without sin*" (Hebrews 4:15, emphasis added). "[God] made Him who knew no sin to be sin for us, that we might become the righteousness of God in Him" (2 Corinthians 5:21).

COVERED BY THE BLOOD: *The Israelites are to take the blood from the lamb and sprinkle it on their doors as an open sign that they belong to God.*

6. THE WHOLE ASSEMBLY OF THE CONGREGATION OF ISRAEL SHALL KILL IT: The entire nation of Israel, that is, every household, was responsible to slaughter a Passover lamb. In this way, each person was forced to recognize that the lamb was being slain for his or her *own* sin; it became a personal sacrifice.

AT TWILIGHT: According to Josephus, it was customary in his day to slaughter the lamb at around 3 P.M. This was precisely the time of day when Christ, God's final Passover Lamb, died (Luke 23:44–46).

7. ON THE TWO DOORPOSTS AND ON THE LINTEL: The Israelites were commanded to put the blood of the sacrifice on the doorposts and lintels of their houses (the top and two sides of the doorway). This was a very bold and forthright sign to all around them that they were covered by the blood. Their sacrifice was not to be done in secret, but openly, letting the world around them know that they were obeying God's commands. Today, our Christian faith should be equally open and forthright, revealing for all to see that we are covered by the blood of the Lamb. "No one, when he has lit a lamp, puts it in a secret place or under a basket, but on a lampstand, that those who come in may see the light" (Luke 11:33).

THE PASSOVER MEAL: *After sacrificing the lamb, the people of Israel are to sit down to a meal—a very unique meal with a unique dress code.*

8. WITH UNLEAVENED BREAD AND WITH BITTER HERBS: Leaven is yeast, and it is often used in Scripture as a symbol of sin. A small amount of yeast affects the entire loaf of bread in the same way that the smallest sin makes a person unable to enter the presence of God. The Israelites were to eat bread without yeast in order to symbolize the fact that Christ, the final Lamb, would one day wash away our sins completely, making us fit to enter God's presence. The bitter herbs were a reminder to the people of the bitterness of their slavery in Egypt. Ironically, they would complain frequently once they were out of Egypt, suggesting that life had been better there than in the wilderness, and this shows us how short our human memory can be. We are to remember on a regular basis how helpless and hopeless we were before Christ redeemed us, and how bitter life is without Him.

11. A BELT ON YOUR WAIST: The Passover was unique not only for its menu, but also for its dress code. The Israelites would ordinarily not wear sandals at a meal, nor would they have a staff in hand, but this meal was to be eaten in haste, not in a leisurely fashion. Furthermore, the Lord commanded His people to eat the meal in clothes that implied a readiness to travel—they were to be *ready* at a moment's notice to get up and leave Egypt. Jesus likewise commanded His followers to be ready for His return: "Watch . . . for you do not know what hour your Lord is coming . . . If the master of the house had known what hour the thief would come, he would have watched and not allowed his house to be broken into. Therefore you also be ready, for the Son of Man is coming at an hour you do not expect" (Matthew 24:42–44; see also Luke 12:39–41).

GOD'S JUDGMENT IS COMING: *The Lord now explains why this sacrifice is so vitally important: His judgment is about to fall upon the Egyptians.*

THE LORD'S PASSOVER: This is where the name originated. The Lord's angel would pass through the nation of Egypt, striking down the firstborn son in each house. But if he saw the blood on the doorposts and lintel, he would "pass over" that house—the Lord's judgment would not fall upon those who were covered in the blood of the Passover lamb. This was a very powerful picture of Christ's sacrifice for our sins: the wrath of God will never fall upon those who are covered in Christ's blood.

12. AGAINST ALL THE GODS OF EGYPT: The Lord had already demonstrated the utter powerlessness of Egypt's gods when He sent the previous nine plagues—many of which specifically mocked Egypt's pantheon. His final plague, however, would demonstrate in one large sweep the utter folly of placing one's faith in anyone or anything but God Himself. The Lord was sending His angel throughout the nation, and there was no power on earth or in hell that could prevent His hand of judgment—no power, that is, except for the means of grace that the Lord had outlined in the Passover stipulations.

13. WHEN I SEE THE BLOOD: As stated in a previous study, when the Lord looks upon His children, He sees us through the blood of Christ, which covers our sins—He does not see our sins. On the other hand, a person whose sins are not covered by the blood of Christ is in imminent danger of God's judgment.

DO NOT FORGET: *The Lord commands the people of Israel to commemorate the Passover feast each year and to diligently teach their children what it means.*

14. A MEMORIAL: It is very important for God's people to *remember*—to remember all that God has done in our lives, and above all, to remember how He saved us and at what cost. "Then [Jesus] said to [His disciples], 'With fervent desire I have desired to eat this Passover with you before I suffer; for I say to you, I will no longer eat of it until it is fulfilled in the kingdom of God.' Then He took the cup, and gave thanks, and said, 'Take this and divide it among yourselves; for I say to you, I will not drink of the fruit of the vine until the kingdom of God comes.' And He took bread, gave thanks and broke it, and gave it to them, saying, 'This is My body which is given for you; do this in remembrance of Me.' Likewise He also took the cup after supper, saying, 'This cup is the new covenant in My blood, which is shed for you'" (Luke 22:15–20).

15. REMOVE LEAVEN FROM YOUR HOUSES: Leaven symbolized sin, as stated previously, and the Lord commanded His people to cleanse their entire lives from it—even to the point of not having any in the house. Anyone who violated this command was to be cut off from Israel. The New Testament similarly commands us to remove the leaven from our own lives: "Therefore purge out the old leaven, that you may be a new lump, since you truly are unleavened. For indeed Christ, our Passover, was sacrificed for us. Therefore let us keep the feast, not with old leaven, nor with the leaven of malice and wickedness, but with the unleavened bread of sincerity and truth" (1 Corinthians 5:7–8). We are further commanded to examine our lives for sin (leaven) prior to partaking of the Lord's Supper, or Communion. "As often as you eat this bread and drink this cup, you proclaim the Lord's death till He comes. Therefore whoever eats this bread or drinks this cup of the Lord in an unworthy manner will be guilty of the body and blood of the Lord. But let a man examine himself, and so let him eat of the bread and drink of the cup. For he who eats and drinks in an unworthy manner eats and drinks judgment to himself, not discerning the Lord's body. For this reason many are weak and sick among you, and many sleep. For if we would judge ourselves, we would not be judged" (1 Corinthians 11:26–31).

26. WHEN YOUR CHILDREN SAY TO YOU: The Lord commanded His people to remember, instituting this Passover as a memorial feast to remind them of what He had done to redeem them. Another vital way of remembering is to teach one's children, and the Scriptures are clear on this point: a father's duty includes teaching his children in the ways of the Lord. "Take heed to yourself, and diligently keep yourself, lest you forget the things your eyes have seen, and lest they depart from your heart all the days of your life. And teach them to your children and your grandchildren ... the LORD said, 'Gather the people to Me, and I will let them hear My words, that they may learn to fear Me all the days they live on the earth, and that they may teach their children'" (Deuteronomy 4:9–10). "Train up a child in the way he should go, and when he is old he will not depart from it" (Proverbs 22:6).

THE DESTROYER COMES: *The Lord sends an angel throughout the land of Egypt, and not one household is spared—except the houses that are covered by the blood.*

29. ALL THE FIRSTBORN IN THE LAND: God's final judgment on Pharaoh covered the entire land of Egypt. It is important to remember that the judgment of God will one day fall upon all men, with equal impartiality. Anyone who is not covered by the blood of Christ shall face God's righteous wrath—from the ruler of the land to the man who sits in the dungeon.

30. THERE WAS A GREAT CRY IN EGYPT: One shudders to imagine the horror of this dark night, as every household throughout Egypt arose in the middle hours to discover death. Yet this is just a small picture of the horror that awaits those who refuse to be covered by God's Passover Lamb. "But the sons of the kingdom will be cast out into outer darkness. There will be weeping and gnashing of teeth" (Matthew 8:12).

31. HE CALLED FOR MOSES AND AARON BY NIGHT: This is the reason the Lord commanded the people to eat the Passover feast in their traveling clothes, as their departure was imminent and very sudden.

46. NOR SHALL YOU BREAK ONE OF ITS BONES: The Passover sacrifice shed its blood, but none of its bones were to be broken. This, too, prefigured Christ. "One of the soldiers pierced His side with a spear, and immediately blood and water came out . . . These things were done that the Scripture should be fulfilled, 'Not one of His bones shall be broken'" (John 19:34–36).

⌒ FIRST IMPRESSIONS ⌒

1. Why were the Israelites commanded to eat the Passover feast with staff in hand? With sandals on? With a belt (which hitched their robes up and out of the way of their feet)?

2. List some of the items on the Passover menu. What did they symbolize? What is the spiritual equivalent of Passover for Christians?

3. Why did the Lord command that the blood of the Passover lamb be sprinkled around the door? What did this symbolize?

4.   *Why did God's wrath fall upon Egypt in this manner? Why did He spare the Israelites?*

∿ Some Key Principles ∿

The Passover lamb is a picture of Christ.

The Lord commanded His people to sacrifice an unblemished lamb and to sprinkle the doorposts with its blood. The lamb was to be a young male, and it was to be cooked in fire rather than boiled. The sacrifice was available to every household; none should be left wanting.

In these ways and many more, the Passover feast in general, and the sacrificial lamb in particular, present us with a detailed picture of the sacrifice of Christ. He is the holy, unblemished Lamb of God, and His death on the cross was the final sacrifice for sin: "The next day John saw Jesus coming toward him, and said, 'Behold! The Lamb of God who takes away the sin of the world!'" (John 1:29). This truth is so important to God's people that we must guard against forgetting who paid for our sins and what that sacrifice cost Him.

God will never pour out His wrath upon those who are covered in the blood.

The Lord's wrath was about to fall upon the Egyptians, and when it came, it fell indiscriminately upon every household in Egypt—except for those that were sprinkled with the blood of the Passover lamb. That blood was an outward sign to the angel that everyone within the house belonged to God, and the angel was not permitted to touch them.

In the same way, Christians are sealed with the blood of Christ; we are eternally protected from God's wrath against sin, and no power can erase that seal. The destroying angel in Egypt did not look upon individual people; he looked upon the blood—or lack of it. When he saw the blood of the lamb, he passed by. When God looks upon His people, He sees the precious blood of His Son, shed for us on the cross to pay the price for our sins. He does not pour out His judgment upon us; His judgment has *already* been poured out—and that judgment fell upon Christ, the final Passover Lamb.

Those who are not covered by the blood of Christ will face eternal judgment.

The preceding principle has a corollary: those who are *not* covered by the blood of the Lamb will indeed face the wrath of God. The destroying angel went throughout the entire land of Egypt, looking for the blood-sprinkled doorposts. He entered every single house that was not sprinkled with blood, slaying the firstborn. There were no exceptions; even cattle were not exempt.

The Lord is no respecter of persons. He does not make special exceptions to this law for people who have lived good lives or given to the poor or observed strict religious rituals. There was only one thing that could prevent the destroyer from slaying the firstborn, and that was the blood of the Passover lamb. There is ultimately only one way to avoid the eternal wrath of God, and that is to be covered by the blood of Christ.

Christians are commanded to live in expectation of Christ's immediate return.

The Israelites were commanded to eat the Passover feast dressed in an unusual fashion: with sandals and walking tunic and staff—ready to leap up and march forth at a moment's notice. This proved necessary that very night, as Pharaoh drove them out of Egypt in the middle hours of darkness.

The Lord Jesus promised that He would return to take His people home, whisking us to heaven just as He suddenly carried His people out of Egypt. Christians are called to live expectantly, ever ready for the sudden and glorious appearing of Jesus Christ. We do not want to be found unprepared: "But of that day and hour no one knows, not even the angels in heaven, nor the Son, but only the Father. Take heed, watch and pray; for you do not know when the time is. It is like a man going to a far country, who left his house and gave authority to his servants, and to each his work, and commanded the doorkeeper to watch. Watch therefore, for you do not know when the master of the house is coming—in the evening, at midnight, at the crowing of the rooster, or in the morning—lest, coming suddenly, he find you sleeping. And what I say to you, I say to all: Watch!" (Mark 13:32–37).

5. What might have happened if an Egyptian family had joined the Passover feast and sprinkled their doorposts with the lamb's blood? What does this suggest about God's grace?

6. What would have happened if an Israelite family had not sprinkled the doorposts with the blood of the lamb? What does this suggest about God's justice?

7. In what ways does the Passover lamb symbolize the person and work of Christ?

8. In what ways does God's judgment on Egypt foreshadow His coming judgment on the entire world? Why were the Israelites supposed to dress like they were ready to leave at any moment? How can Christians be similarly prepared to leave this world at any moment?

⸲ Taking It Personally ⸲

9. Are you living with the expectancy of Christ's imminent return? How can you keep that expectation in mind this week?

10. Are your sins covered by the sacrificial death of Jesus Christ? If not, what is preventing you from believing in Him?

~ II ~
REBELLION

~ HISTORICAL BACKGROUND ~

The Israelites had been traveling through the wilderness for about a year, and during that time they had witnessed the Lord's immense power and miraculous intervention again and again. One miracle in particular had taken place twice a day for that entire time: the miracle of manna. Each morning and evening, the Lord rained down a unique wafer-like substance called *manna*, a nutritious and tasty food direct from the Lord Himself.

This wonder was profound. The food was so nourishing that the people did not need to eat anything else whatsoever. They never got hungry, and it kept them healthy—and best of all, it tasted good, like wafers made with honey. They did not need to go out and hunt for it or gather it from bushes; they merely stepped outside their tents and picked it up off the ground. The Lord delivered it right to their doorsteps! Best of all, there was always more than enough for everyone, so nobody ever went hungry or unsatisfied. What was left over would melt away in the morning sun—yet the manna that was collected on the day before Sabbath would miraculously *not* disappear, but would instead sustain the people on their day of rest. There was so much of God's love in the manna that it is hard to believe that anyone would have complained.

But that is just what the people did. A few people started grumbling about their meat-less diet, remembering the varied foods they had enjoyed in Egypt (while conveniently forgetting the dreadful slave labor with which they had earned it). The murmuring soon spread from a few to many, and before long the entire nation of Israel was rebelling against the Lord—just because He hadn't rained down some meat along with the manna! As inconceivable as this may sound, it is no different from rebellion among God's people today, a sin that God detests as much as the sin of witchcraft.

~ READING NUMBERS 11:1–35 ~

THE PEOPLE COMPLAIN: *The Israelites have been away from Egypt for about a year, and the Lord has been miraculously feeding them twice a day. But they grow dissatisfied.*

1. WHEN THE PEOPLE COMPLAINED: The Israelites had been away from Egypt for about a year as this passage opens. But their complaining had begun very soon after leaving Egypt, when they saw Pharaoh's army behind them, and it continued for the next forty years.

FOR THE LORD HEARD IT: We must remember that the Lord hears the words of our mouths, and He has promised to hold us accountable for what we speak. "But I say to you that for every idle word men may speak, they will give account of it in the day of judgment. For by your words you will be justified, and by your words you will be condemned" (Matthew 12:36–37).

HIS ANGER WAS AROUSED: The people's faithless response was inexcusable. Though they had repeatedly seen the Lord's miraculous work, they responded to their current circumstances by grumbling rather than by trusting God. The Lord's anger is not aroused by our physiological responses to circumstances, but rather by our attitude in the midst of those circumstances. At one point in their travels, the people of Israel were thirsty, as we saw in a previous study. They were not wrong to feel thirst; neither was it wrong to desire water. They were wrong when they chose to forget all that the Lord had already done for them and to accuse Him of not caring about them. This is the fundamental element of complaining: imputing false motives to God and choosing to overlook His past victories in our lives, focusing instead on what He has apparently failed to do (based on what *we* want Him to do) in the present situation. It is a sin of ingratitude and can lead to the sin of blasphemy, imputing evil to God.

THE FIRE OF THE LORD BURNED AMONG THEM: God sometimes sent strong discipline upon His people when they grumbled. Ingratitude and complaining are sins that we should take seriously (since God certainly does).

3. TABERAH: Meaning "burning."

4. THE MIXED MULTITUDE: There were Egyptians and others who left Egypt with the people of Israel.

LUSTING FOR MEAT: *The Lord had been providing manna twice a day, and it was more than enough for them to survive while in the wilderness. But the people were still not satisfied.*

INTENSE CRAVING: The Hebrew phrase is literally "desire desire." The people were lusting for meat.

WHO WILL GIVE US MEAT?: This is an indirect insult to the Lord, for the answer to the question is "God will!" He had provided them with water, food, shade from the sun, light in the darkness, and every other physical need on their journey. In the face of this accusatory question, the Lord must certainly have felt as insulted as he did over King David's lust: "And if that had been too little, I also would have given you much more!" (2 Samuel 12:8).

5. WE REMEMBER THE FISH WHICH WE ATE FREELY IN EGYPT: But they had evidently forgotten the horrible cost they had paid to get those foods. The Lord had made it clear to Israel that if they obeyed Him, they would only be in the wilderness a relatively short time. (Of course, this was prior to the final rebellion of the ten spies. Due to that future act of rebellion, they would end up remaining in the land of Canaan for the rest of their lives.) They were briefly "making do" without meat until they arrived at the land that would flow with milk and honey.

6. NOTHING AT ALL EXCEPT THIS MANNA BEFORE OUR EYES: The Lord had been miraculously feeding the Israelites twice a day for a year. Each morning and each evening—except on Sabbath days—the Lord rained down food from the heavens. The Israelites had only to step outside their tents to gather it—and it even tasted good. But notice the wording of this complaint: "nothing at all except *this manna*." It expressed contempt for God's good gift, and it also suggested that the people were literally fed up with it. Grumbling, as we have seen already, is a form of rebellion against God, and it grows out of ingratitude.

8. GROUND IT ON MILLSTONES OR BEAT IT IN THE MORTAR: Manna had the added benefit of many uses. It evidently served equally well as flour and could undoubtedly be used in a wide variety of dishes. Of course, there was not an abundance of other ingredients available, but that situation was only intended to be temporary, and the manna was more than enough to carry them through the wilderness. Soldiers, sailors, explorers, and many others have subsisted longer on less.

MOSES IS FED UP: *The people are hungry for meat, but Moses is completely fed up with their constant complaining. The Lord, too, is displeased.*

10. MOSES ALSO WAS DISPLEASED: As we saw in a previous study, our complaining can bring harm to others around us. The complaints about the manna cast aspersions on Moses' leadership, and he was becoming discouraged.

11. WHY HAVE YOU AFFLICTED YOUR SERVANT?: Complaining breeds complaining, just as encouragement breeds encouragement. Moses was so moved by the people's ingratitude that he, in turn, poured out a lament before the Lord. His feelings were understandable, yet he, too, was accusing the Lord of false motives. God had not "afflicted" Moses with leadership; his role brought with it great blessings and privileges, not the least of which was speaking face-to-face with the Lord as a man speaks to a friend. This alone was enough to prove that Moses had found favor with the Lord, yet at this moment he was accusing Him of the opposite.

13. THEY WEEP ALL OVER ME: This is a wonderful depiction of the Israelites' whining. They were crying like spoiled children, throwing a tantrum because they couldn't have what they wanted for supper.

14. I AM NOT ABLE TO BEAR ALL THESE PEOPLE ALONE: This was actually quite true, but Moses was losing sight for the moment of the fact that he did *not* bear the burden alone—the Lord bore it for him. This is the mark of a person who is trying to accomplish the Lord's work in his own strength; when we do this, discouragement and weariness quickly set in. On the flip side, this incident also demonstrates how people's complaints can be wearying to their leaders.

15. PLEASE KILL ME HERE AND NOW: Elijah prayed a similar prayer when he felt alone (1 Kings 19:4, 9–10). We are indeed fortunate that the Lord does not grant everything we ask for.

17. THAT YOU MAY NOT BEAR IT YOURSELF ALONE: The Lord showed His mercy toward Moses by giving him seventy men to assist him in the work of leading the people. The Israelites were a vast multitude, more than six hundred thousand strong, and the duties of leadership must have been a constant burden. So God graciously gave Moses other men to whom Moses could delegate parts of his responsibility.

SATISFYING THEIR LUSTS: *The Lord grants the people's request for meat—to the uttermost. He allows them to satisfy their lust and to discover that lust is never truly satisfied.*

18. YOU SHALL EAT MEAT: There are times when the Lord will give us exactly what we ask for—but He will at the same time send leanness into our souls. The people's complaining was similar to Balaam's repeatedly asking God for permission to curse the Israelites. The Lord had already said no, but Balaam was motivated by his own fleshly desires. God eventually gave him the desired permission, but it led to an ungodly end. The result was the same for Israel: "They soon forgot His works; they did not wait for His counsel, but lusted exceedingly in the wilderness, and tested God in the desert. And He gave them their request, but sent leanness into their soul" (Psalm 106:13–15).

20. UNTIL IT COMES OUT OF YOUR NOSTRILS: The people's lust for meat was so unbridled that the Lord determined to satisfy their lust—to the point that the very meat they had craved became loathsome. This is a common consequence that comes from gratifying the lusts of the flesh. Lusts of any description, when gratified, soon cease to be pleasurable and become merely a disgusting addiction.

YOU HAVE DESPISED THE LORD: At the foundation of complaining is a hatred for the Lord. The people were effectively saying that they hated God and His provisions, and they would have preferred to remain slaves to the Egyptians.

23. HAS THE LORD'S ARM BEEN SHORTENED?: The Lord's patience and mercy toward His people were truly remarkable. He showed His faithfulness again and again; but they forgot again and again; they rebelled again and again—yet He continued to patiently explain that He had been faithful in the past and would be in the future.

SEVENTY PROPHETS: *The Lord commands Moses to appoint seventy elders from Israel to assist him in his leadership duties. These men are suddenly filled with God's Spirit.*

29. OH, THAT ALL THE LORD'S PEOPLE WERE PROPHETS: Moses demonstrated once again the meekness of his character. He was not threatened by the prophesying of the other men; on the contrary, he rejoiced that the Lord had poured out His Spirit upon them (for the purpose of equipping them to lead His people). His desire looked forward to the day when all of God's people would have His Spirit within them. Thus, Moses' comment here anticipates the New Covenant. (See Ezekiel 36:22–27 and Jeremiah 31:31–37 for more on the New Covenant.) Despite all this, however, the people of Moses' day would soon rise up against him and accuse him of lording it over them.

31. TWO CUBITS: That is, about three feet. Countless quail had blown in from the sea by a wind that God had sent out. They evidently were fluttering to and fro just above the ground.

32. THE PEOPLE STAYED UP ALL THAT DAY, ALL NIGHT, AND ALL THE NEXT DAY: The people went into a frenzy as they ran about, clubbing birds to satisfy their appetites. It is a frightening picture.

TEN HOMERS: Approximately sixty to seventy bushels—and that was the *least* anyone gathered. The Lord was more than providing—He was sending a surfeit.

33. WHILE THE MEAT WAS STILL BETWEEN THEIR TEETH: This is a graphic depiction of the people gratifying their physical lust. There is no suggestion that the meat even tasted good or was in any way satisfying; it was merely "between their teeth," being chewed and swallowed in a gluttonous food fest.

34. KIBROTH HATTAAVAH: "Graves of Craving." God sent a severe plague in response to the people's lust. As a result, many died on account of their rebellious ingratitude and sinful cravings. "Each one is tempted when he is drawn away by his own desires and enticed. Then, when desire has conceived, it gives birth to sin; and sin, when it is full-grown, brings forth death" (James 1:14–15).

MIRIAM AND AARON REBEL: *The prophesying of the seventy elders apparently led Miriam and Aaron to be jealous of Moses' authority. Their dissatisfaction is a precursor to open rebellion.*

1. MIRIAM AND AARON: Moses' sister and brother. This revolt must have been all the more painful for Moses, since he was betrayed by his closest family relations.

THE ETHIOPIAN WOMAN WHOM HE HAD MARRIED: Although the term "Ethiopian" could have been used concerning Zipporah, Moses' first wife, it seems more likely that Moses had remarried after the death of Zipporah. The marriage to the Ethiopian woman had been recent and was probably just an excuse for rebelling against Moses; the real issue was Moses' role as the Lord's spokesman. Since Miriam is mentioned first, she probably was the instigator of the attack against Moses.

2. HAS THE LORD INDEED SPOKEN ONLY THROUGH MOSES?: The true motivation for this rebellion appears to have begun when the seventy men prophesied (Numbers 11:25). Rather than rejoicing that the Lord had extended His Spirit to others, as Moses had done, Miriam and Aaron began to view Moses' Spirit-filled leadership with contempt. Miriam and Aaron apparently wanted to be included, claiming that God had spoken to them in the same way that He had spoken to Moses.

THE LORD HEARD IT: Once again we are reminded that the Lord is listening to the things we say. (See the commentary on Numbers 11:1.)

3. VERY HUMBLE: This statement is sometimes used to argue that Moses could not have written the book of Numbers, since it is thought unlikely that he would have boasted in his own humility. However, the Holy Spirit certainly could inspire Moses to make an accurate statement about himself, probably against his own natural inclination. In this context, Moses was asserting that he had done nothing to provoke this attack by Miriam and Aaron.

4. SUDDENLY: The Lord's wrath fell upon the people suddenly and without warning. This is a terrifying situation, yet the New Testament warns us that the Lord's wrath will finally fall upon the earth just as suddenly. "The day of the Lord will come as a thief in the night, in which the heavens will pass away with a great noise, and the elements will melt with fervent heat; both the earth and the works that are in it will be burned up" (2 Peter 3:10).

8. I SPEAK WITH HIM FACE TO FACE: Moses was more than just a spokesman for the Lord—he was the Lord's *friend*. The Lord did not speak to Moses through visions and dreams, but plainly and directly. In this, Moses was incredibly privileged.

WHY THEN WERE YOU NOT AFRAID: It is a very serious matter to rebel against the Lord's appointed leaders—both inside and outside of the church. (See Hebrews 13:17.) The Scriptures make it abundantly clear that Christians are to submit themselves to people in authority—even in a secular and ungodly society. "Therefore submit yourselves to every ordinance of man for the Lord's sake, whether to the king as supreme, or to governors, as to those who are sent by him for the punishment of evildoers and for the praise of those who do good. For this is the will of God, that by doing good you may put to silence the ignorance of foolish men" (1 Peter 2:13–15).

MIRIAM BECOMES A LEPER: *The Lord strikes Miriam immediately with leprosy, and she is removed from the camp. But He also shows His mercy and grace.*

10. SUDDENLY MIRIAM BECAME LEPROUS: Miriam was evidently the instigator of this rebellion. She had sinned openly and publicly, and therefore the results of that rebellion would be equally public. Lepers were utterly shunned by all the people and were forced to live outside the camp in a place of dishonor. Leprosy, like the sin of grumbling, was very contagious and deadly.

11. IN WHICH WE HAVE SINNED: God's people must understand the gravity of rebellion. To speak evil against the leaders whom God has appointed is a grievous sin.

14. IF HER FATHER HAD BUT SPIT IN HER FACE: If a father spat in the face of his daughter, it would indicate that she had somehow disgraced the family name. The Lord was saying that Miriam's rebellious spirit was a disgrace to the name of God. Grumbling and rebellion discredit God's name before the world around us, because such actions demonstrate emphatically that God's own people do not respect Him.

AFTERWARD SHE MAY BE RECEIVED AGAIN: Nevertheless, the Lord once again displayed His grace. He did not strike Miriam dead, as He would have been justified in doing; neither did He leave her a leper. She did remain segregated from the rest of the people for seven days. Only afterward was she fully restored into the camp.

☞ FIRST IMPRESSIONS ☜

1. *If you had been traveling in the desert for a year, eating manna twice a day, what would your attitude be toward your diet?*

2. What led the people of Israel to complain about the lack of meat? What does this reveal about complaining?

3. Why did the Lord give the people meat "until it came out of their nostrils"? What does this reveal about lust?

4. What led Miriam and Aaron to rebel against Moses? How did their attitude differ from Moses' attitude?

⌁ Some Key Principles ⌁

Choose to be content where the Lord has placed you.

The Lord had led His people into the wilderness, a desert region devoid of food and water. He wanted them to live there for a short time in order to show them how He would provide for all their needs, and He rained manna on them twice a day and provided water miraculously. But the people grew tired of manna; they complained about eating "nothing at all except this manna before our eyes" (Numbers 11:6), and they began to complain about not having meat.

This demonstrates an important principle of happiness: we *choose* whether or not we will be content. Contentment comes when we remember to be grateful for what the Lord has given us. If the Israelites had remembered each day to praise the Lord for His miraculous provision of food and water—focusing on the good things they *did* have—

they would not have focused on the meat they *didn't* have. They would have been content, and the Lord would have been glorified.

Paul wrote, "I have learned in whatever state I am, to be content" (Philippians 4:11). This is an excellent pattern for the body of Christ to emulate, because "godliness with contentment is great gain. For we brought nothing into this world, and it is certain we can carry nothing out. And having food and clothing, with these we shall be content. But those who desire to be rich fall into temptation and a snare, and into many foolish and harmful lusts which drown men in destruction and perdition" (1 Timothy 6:6–9).

Lust is never truly satisfied.

The Israelites told themselves they could be completely satisfied *if only* they had some meat. This is the nature of lust—it is an "if only" mind-set, focusing on the one thing we don't have rather than on the many things we do have. "*If only* I had this, I'd be happy"; "*If only* I had that, I'd be fulfilled." Lust is the natural outgrowth of a lack of contentment.

There are two problems with lust: it leads us to disobey God's commands in trying to satisfy our sinful desires, and it can never be satisfied. Even if we do gain the one thing that was missing, it will not bring us lasting happiness. There will only be another missing thing in back of it, another "if only" to replace the present one. Lust compels us to do anything and everything to satisfy it, and it inevitably leads us to violate the Lord's commands. The Israelites indulged their lust for meat, and it led them to rebel against the Lord.

Peter warned the New Testament church to refrain from fulfilling the lust of the flesh: "Beloved, I beg you as sojourners and pilgrims, abstain from fleshly lusts which war against the soul" (1 Peter 2:11).

Rebellion is like the sin of witchcraft.

"For rebellion is as the sin of witchcraft" (1 Samuel 15:23). The Lord's response to rebellion among the Israelites was swift and strong. Miriam was stricken instantly with leprosy, Korah and his followers were swallowed up by the earth, and fire rained from heaven and burned a portion of the Israelite camp on another occasion. The Lord hates a rebellious spirit, just as He hates witchcraft.

The reason for this is that a rebellious spirit is actually the same in its essence as witchcraft and idolatry. When we grumble about the Lord's provision in our lives, we are rebelling against His leadership and authority. When we rebel against the Lord, we are setting ourselves up in His place as lord of our lives. This is the same sin that Satan committed when he declared himself to be equal with God.

God has pronounced woe on all who rebel against Him—even His own: "'Woe to the rebellious children,' says the LORD, 'who take counsel, but not of Me, and who devise plans, but not of My Spirit, that they may add sin to sin'" (Isaiah 30:1). Worse, he considers every rebel his *foe*—and actually fights them. "But they rebelled and grieved His Holy Spirit; so He turned Himself against them as an enemy, and He fought against them" (Isaiah 63:10).

⤳ DIGGING DEEPER ⤶

5. *Why were the Israelites not content with manna? What is needed to find contentment?*

6. *How does lust differ from normal and righteous desires? How did the Israelites' lust for meat differ from physical hunger?*

7. *In what ways is a complaining spirit the same as a rebellious spirit? How can one person's grumbling lead to open rebellion?*

8. Why does God hate rebellion? Explain in your own words how rebellion is like the sin of witchcraft.

⤳ Taking It Personally ⤳

9. Are you content where the Lord has placed you? If not, what must you change in yourself to find contentment? (Remember, contentment comes from a change of heart, not a change of circumstances.)

10. Do you have a complaining spirit or a submissive spirit? How do submissiveness and contentment reinforce one another?

NOTES AND PRAYER REQUESTS

SECTION 4:

SUMMARY

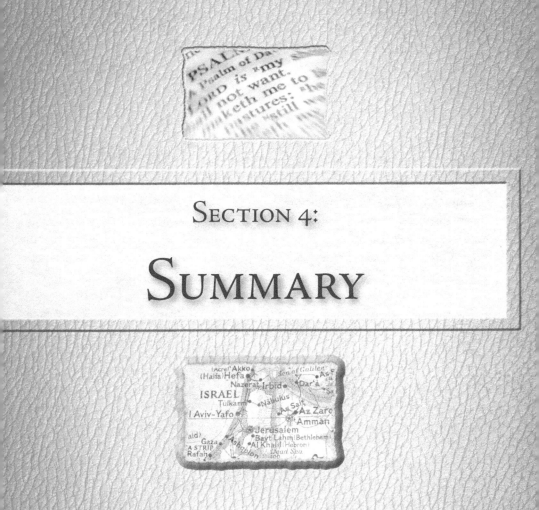

SUMMARY AND REVIEW

⌖ LOOKING BACK ⌖

In the preceding eleven studies, we have covered an important period of Israel's history in just a few studies. There is much more in the Pentateuch concerning Israel's wanderings in the wilderness, yet in these few glimpses we have seen again and again that the Lord is faithful to His promises, and He always provides for His people. We have also seen the sad truth that God's people are quick to become discontented, quick to rebel against the Lord's leadership. In fact, Israel's rebellion against God was a recurring theme, practically from their first day as freed slaves. Yet from their story, we can glean some valuable principles that, if heeded, will mean the difference between God's frown and His favor upon our lives.

Here are a few of the major themes we have found. There are many more that we don't have room to reiterate, so take some time to review the earlier studies—or better still, to meditate upon the passages in Scripture that we have covered. As you do, remember to ask the Holy Spirit to give you wisdom and insight into His Word.

⌖ SOME KEY PRINCIPLES ⌖

We must not harden our hearts against God's Word.

Pharaoh repeatedly refused to obey God's commands to let the Israelites leave Egypt, yet the Lord continued to give him opportunities to repent. Eventually, however, the Lord gave him over to his hardness of heart, allowing him to remain in stubborn rebellion.

The same principle is true today for the lost world around us. We are living in the day of grace, when salvation is freely available to all who believe, but that day will not last forever. The day is coming when the time for repentance will be past. In that dark day, all who have rejected Christ will be cast out of the presence of God for all eternity.

It is a very dangerous matter to resist God's grace. Each time a person refuses to repent, repentance becomes more difficult. Those who need to repent must do it *now*: "For He says: 'In an acceptable time I have heard you, and in the day of salvation I have helped you.' Behold, now is the accepted time; behold, now is the day of salvation" (2 Corinthians 6:2).

Never forget what the Lord has done.

The people of Israel had seen many amazing miracles as the Lord demonstrated His power and determination to set them free from slavery. He had sent ten plagues that devastated Egypt, while leaving the Israelites unharmed. He had spoken to them through Moses, predicting that Pharaoh would drive them out of Egypt, heavily laden with gold and silver—and it had happened exactly as promised. Yet when the first setback occurred, they instantly forgot all those signs and wonders and accused God of betraying them.

This is a characteristic that is common to fallen human nature. We rejoice when the Lord blesses us, giving Him glory and thanks for His loving intervention in our lives. But then something goes wrong, some unexpected threat arises—and we are immediately filled with fear and doubt. We wonder if the Lord has abandoned us, or we simply forget to trust Him and try instead to solve the matter by our own power.

It is vital that we remember what the Lord has done in our lives, so we don't become fearful when circumstances go against us. If the Lord was faithful in the past, we can be confident that He will be faithful in the future. "Beware that you do not forget the LORD your God by not keeping His commandments, His judgments, and His statutes which I command you today" (Deuteronomy 8:11). "Bless the LORD, O my soul, and forget not all His benefits" (Psalm 103:2).

We are to fear God alone, not man.

Pharaoh was the most powerful man in the most powerful nation on earth. His army was feared around the known world, and they were equipped with the latest technologies and the best training. The Israelites, on the other hand, were newly released slaves with no military experience and no chariots. It is no wonder they were frightened when they looked behind them and saw the great dust cloud of Pharaoh's army bearing down.

But the greatest army on earth is no match for the power of God. The Lord led Pharaoh's army into the Red Sea and then plucked off the wheels of their chariots as simply as a man snaps a toothpick. At the same time, He led His people *through* the sea on dry ground. They did not even get their feet wet!

Our tendency is to focus on what we can see, to believe the evidence of our senses. But the Lord calls us to walk by faith, not by sight, and to rely fully on His unlimited power and His faithfulness.

"In God I have put my trust; I will not be afraid. What can man do to me?" (Psalm 56:11). "For He Himself has said, 'I will never leave you nor forsake you.' So we may boldly say: 'The LORD is my helper; I will not fear. What can man do to me?'" (Hebrews 13:5–6).

The Ten Commandments are summarized by the two greatest commandments.

The Lord summarized His moral law for the people of Israel in the Ten Commandments. In the New Testament, Jesus summarized them even further.

A young man asked Jesus, "Teacher, which is the great commandment in the law?" Jesus said to him, '*You shall love the Lord your God with all your heart, with all your soul, and with all your mind.*' This is the first and great commandment. And the second is like it: '*You shall love your neighbor as yourself.*' On these two commandments hang all the Law and the Prophets" (Matthew 22:36–40).

The Ten Commandments themselves fall into these two categories. Some of them spell out what it means to love God with all our hearts, souls, and minds, while others give practical ways of loving our neighbors as we do ourselves. These two principles summarize what it means to live a godly life. Keeping the Law will not bring us redemption for sin—only the death of Christ, God's Passover Lamb, can accomplish that—but Christians *are* called to put these two principles into action in all areas of life.

"For the commandments, 'You shall not commit adultery,' 'You shall not murder,' 'You shall not steal,' 'You shall not bear false witness,' 'You shall not covet,' and if there is any other commandment, are all summed up in this saying, namely, 'You shall love your neighbor as yourself.' Love does no harm to a neighbor; therefore love is the fulfillment of the law" (Romans 13:9–10).

Do not dabble in the occult.

Balaam was just one of many false prophets in Canaan during his day. These people used various forms of magic and sorcery to speak with false gods (demons) and to "tap into" the power of the spirit realm. What they didn't know, however, was that they were not interacting with any gods at all, but rather with the power of Satan.

Interest in the occult is on the rise in Western society today, and even Christians are being lured into dabbling with "spirit guides," "channeling," horoscopes, praying to angels, and other elements of magic. These things are not innocent toys to play with, nor are they legitimate powers that mankind has at his disposal. They are forms of sorcery, and the power behind them is the devil.

God forbids His people from any contact with such things. "There shall not be found among you anyone who . . . practices witchcraft, or a soothsayer, or one who interprets omens, or a sorcerer, or one who conjures spells, or a medium, or a spiritist, or one who calls up the dead. For all who do these things are an abomination to the LORD" (Deuteronomy 18:10–12).

Rebellion is like the sin of witchcraft.

"For rebellion is as the sin of witchcraft" (1 Samuel 15:23). The Lord's response to rebellion among the Israelites was swift and strong. Miriam was stricken instantly with leprosy, Korah and his followers were swallowed up by the earth, and fire rained from heaven and burned a portion of the Israelite camp on another occasion. The Lord hates a rebellious spirit, just as He hates witchcraft.

The reason for this is that a rebellious spirit is actually the same in its essence as witchcraft and idolatry. When we grumble and complain about the Lord's provision in our lives, we are rebelling against His leadership and authority. When we rebel against the Lord, we are setting ourselves up in His place as lord of our lives. This is the same sin that Satan committed when he declared himself to be equal with God.

God has pronounced woe on all who rebel against Him—even His own people: "'Woe to the rebellious children,' says the LORD, 'who take counsel, but not of Me, and who devise plans, but not of My Spirit, that they may add sin to sin'" (Isaiah 30:1). Worse, he considers every rebel his *foe*—and actually fights them: "But they rebelled and grieved His Holy Spirit; so He turned Himself against them as an enemy, and He fought against them" (Isaiah 63:10).

God's people are to be of good courage.

God's Word frequently commands us to "be of good courage" and "fear not." These are commands, not suggestions or mere words of encouragement. The emotion of fear can come upon us at times whether we will it or not, but what we do with that fear is a matter of our will, a matter of obedience to God's command.

Joshua and Caleb saw the very same giants that the other ten spies saw. They examined the same walled cities, observed the same trained enemy armies—yet they came to a radically different conclusion. The reason was that Joshua and Caleb deliberately resisted and overcame their fear, while the other ten fell prey to it.

We resist fear by consciously focusing our minds on the promises and character of God, not on the seemingly insurmountable problems that we face. We also resist fear by remembering the many ways in which God has been faithful in the past, and by choosing to trust Him to continue to be faithful in the future. In a phrase, we resist fear simply by *choosing* to trust God instead.

Contentment is a choice.

The Lord had led His people into the wilderness, a desert region devoid of food and water. He wanted them to live there for a short time in order to show them how He would provide for all their needs, and He rained manna on them twice a day and provided water miraculously. But the people grew tired of manna; they complained about eating "nothing at all except this manna before our eyes" (Numbers 11:6), and they began to complain about not having meat.

This demonstrates an important principle of happiness: we *choose* whether or not we will be content. Contentment comes when we remember to be grateful for what the Lord has given us. If the Israelites had remembered each day to praise the Lord for His miraculous provision of food and water—focusing on the good things they *did* have—they would not have focused on the meat they *didn't* have. They would have been content, and the Lord would have been glorified. Paul wrote, "I have learned in whatever state I am, to be content" (Philippians 4:11), a very good pattern for God's people to emulate. Why? Because "godliness with contentment is great gain. For we brought nothing into this world, and it is certain we can carry nothing out. And having food and clothing, with these we shall be content. But those who desire to be rich fall into temptation and a snare, and into many foolish and harmful lusts which drown men in destruction and perdition" (1 Timothy 6:6–9).

⌁ DIGGING DEEPER ⌁

1. *What are some of the more important things you have learned from Exodus and Numbers?*

2.   Which of the concepts or principles have you found most encouraging? Which have been most challenging?

3.   What aspects of "walking with God" are you already doing in your life? Which areas need strengthening?

4.   Which of the characters that we've studied have you felt the most attracted to? How might you emulate that person in your own life?

⌁ Taking It Personally ⌁

5.   Have you embraced Jesus Christ as your Lord and Savior and taken a definite stand for Him? Have you accepted His free gift of salvation? If not, why not?

6.   What areas of your personal life have been most convicted during this study? What exact things will you do to address these convictions? Be specific.

7.   What have you learned about the character of God during this study? How has this insight affected your worship or prayer life?

8.   List below the specific things you want to see God do in your life in the coming month. List also the things you intend to change in your own life in that time. Return to this list in one month and hold yourself accountable to fulfill these things.

If you would like to continue in your study of the Old Testament, read the next title in this series: *Finally in the Land: Canaan and the Kinsman Redeemer.*